THE DISCIPLINED CEO

MASTERING PERSISTENCE, FOCUS, AND RESILIENCE

JASON MILLER

CHRIS O'BYRNE,
TONY DURSO, DANIEL HAMMOND,
DR. TRAVIS HEARNE, LUBA SAKHARUK,
CHAD BRUCKNER, JON HOERAUF

ISBN: 978-1-957217-33-8 (paperback)
ISBN: 978-1-957217-34-5 (hardback)
ISBN: 978-1-957217-35-2 (ebook)

CONTENTS

Precision Focus: Discipline Lessons from an Army Sniper

Jason Miller

In this chapter, I share insights from my experience as an army sniper, a role that exemplifies the utmost in precision, focus, and disciplined decision-making. These skills, honed in the rigor of military service, have profound applications in business leadership.

The life of a sniper is defined by thorough planning, unwavering focus, and a steadfast commitment to accuracy. Remarkably, these same principles are instrumental in elevating your effectiveness in business leadership.

We'll cover three critical themes:

1. **Precision**: Similar to how snipers accurately align their shots, a business leader must apply precision in their strategic initiatives. This section will explore how meticulous planning, execution, and measurement are crucial in business, mirroring the sniper's approach.

2. **Focus**: Renowned for their ability to maintain focus in diverse and challenging situations, snipers offer

lessons in concentration that are invaluable in the business environment, where distractions are pervasive. We will discuss techniques snipers use to sustain focus and adapt these methods to enhance clarity and concentration in business settings.

3. **Disciplined Decision-Making**: The decision-making process of a sniper is characterized by discipline and critical analysis, often under significant pressure. This mirrors the complex decision-making scenarios faced by business leaders. This segment will delve into applying a sniper's disciplined approach to making informed, strategic decisions in business.

Upon concluding this chapter, you will gain insight into how the discipline, precision, and focus cultivated in an army sniper's life are relevant and essential for mastering the nuances of business leadership. This exploration aims to inspire and provide practical guidance for enhancing decision-making capabilities, strategic planning, and overall leadership efficacy.

THE SNIPER'S CRAFT: AN OVERVIEW

Exploring the role of an army sniper reveals a world where skill, mental strength, and strategic thinking are crucial. Being a sniper is much more than being an expert shooter; it involves a range of complex duties and skills that are often misunderstood.

The primary task of a sniper is precision shooting—hitting targets accurately from long distances. This ability is not just a natural talent; it's developed through intense, ongoing training and a strong focus on accuracy. But a sniper's job goes beyond just shooting. They are also responsible for gathering important information about the enemy and the environment, playing a vital role in the planning and success of military missions. Their skill in staying hidden and blending into their surroundings, sometimes for long periods, is critical for gathering intelligence and preparing for the perfect shot.

The qualities that define a sniper are what makes their role so unique. Precision for a sniper means carefully selecting the right target, time, and method. This level of precision comes from detailed planning and deep knowledge of various factors, like ballistics and environmental conditions. Patience is another crucial quality of a sniper. The ability to wait, sometimes in harsh conditions, for the right moment to act is a sign of their discipline and resilience.

A sniper's focus is also essential. They must maintain concentration in different and often stressful situations. This involves mental endurance and staying focused on the mission despite distractions or internal pressures. Finally, making decisions under pressure is a critical skill for a sniper. They often have to make quick, life-changing decisions in high-pressure situations. This requires not only staying calm but also being able to understand a situation and make intelligent decisions quickly.

As we go further into this chapter, we will explore how these sniper qualities—precision, patience, focus, and decision-making under pressure—are just as important in business leadership. These attributes, developed in the demanding environment of military service, offer valuable lessons and practical applications for today's business leaders.

PRECISION: THE HALLMARK OF SUCCESS

In the world of an army sniper, precision is not just a skill; it's a fundamental principle that guides every action, decision, and shot. We need to see precision through a sniper's lens to understand this. It's about choosing the exact moment, the perfect angle, and the ideal conditions to take a shot that can't afford to miss. This level of precision is achieved through intense training, deep knowledge, and an acute understanding of every variable, from wind speed to the target's movement.

Now, let's draw a parallel to the business world. Here, precision is equally critical but manifests differently. In business, precision means making decisions and strategies that are well-calculated, targeted, and timed. It's about aligning resources, efforts, and objectives to maximize impact and minimize waste. This kind of precision in decision-making can mean the difference between a thriving business and one that struggles to find its footing.

Consider the example of a technology company launching a new product to bring this concept to life. Much like a sniper, the company's leadership team must carefully assess the market, understand consumer needs, and time the launch perfectly. Every aspect, from the product's features to the marketing campaign, must be precisely tailored to meet the target audience's desires and the market's demands. A misstep in timing or a miscalculation in the product's appeal could result in failure, just as a sniper missing their mark could have serious consequences.

Another example can be seen in the financial sector. Investment decisions made by financial analysts share a striking resemblance to a sniper's precision. Analysts must meticulously evaluate market trends, company performance, and economic indicators to make investment choices. A well-timed, precisely calculated investment decision can lead to significant profits, while a poorly judged one can lead to substantial losses.

In both these cases, the common thread is the meticulous attention to detail and the careful calibration of actions to achieve a specific, well-defined goal. This precision approach, borrowed from the discipline of a sniper, can drive success in the high-stakes business world. It's about making every move count, every decision matter, and aligning every effort towards a clear, precise objective. Precision, in essence, is the hallmark of success, both on the battlefield and in the boardroom.

THE ART OF FOCUS

In a sniper's intense and high-stakes world, maintaining focus over extended periods is not just a skill; it's a necessity. This unparalleled level of focus sets snipers apart and enables them to perform their duties with exceptional precision. Understanding how they achieve and sustain this focus provides invaluable insights, particularly when applied to the business environment.

A sniper's focus is a blend of mental stamina and an acute awareness of their surroundings. They train themselves to stay alert and attentive, often for hours, while remaining motionless. This focus demands mastery over the mind, an ability to control wandering thoughts, and a resilience to physical discomfort. It's a meditative state, where the sniper becomes one with their environment, fully immersed in the task at hand.

Translating this into the business world, maintaining focus over long periods is equally critical. In an age where distractions are constant and demands are high, the ability to concentrate on a task can make a significant difference in productivity and the quality of work. Business leaders, much like snipers, need to develop this deep focus to navigate complex projects, make strategic decisions, and lead their teams effectively.

Several techniques can be borrowed from snipers to cultivate this kind of focus in a business setting. First, it's about creating an environment conducive to concentration. Just as a sniper selects a position where they can remain undisturbed and alert, a business professional needs to make a workspace that minimizes distractions. This could mean setting aside specific times for deep work, using technology mindfully, or even restructuring the physical workspace.

Another technique is the practice of mindfulness and mental discipline. Snipers often use breathing techniques and mental exercises to stay calm and focused. Similarly, business leaders can benefit from mindfulness practices, such as meditation or focused breathing, to improve concentration and mental clarity. These practices enhance the ability to focus, manage stress, and make clear-headed decisions.

Lastly, the sniper's art of focus involves breaking down tasks into manageable parts. This approach can be applied in business by setting clear, achievable goals and milestones. By focusing on one task at a time and breaking larger projects into smaller steps, business professionals can maintain a high level of focus and avoid feeling overwhelmed.

In summary, the art of focus is a skill that can be cultivated and honed. By adopting techniques from the disciplined world of snipers, business leaders and professionals can enhance their ability to concentrate, leading to improved decision-making, efficiency, and overall performance in the fast-paced business environment.

PATIENCE AND PERSEVERANCE

In the meticulous world of a sniper, patience is more than a virtue; it is an essential element of their routine. A sniper's mission often involves waiting for the perfect moment to take a shot, which might come after hours or even days of vigilant waiting. This waiting game requires an extraordinary level of patience and mental resilience. It's not just about staying still; it's about maintaining a high level of concentration during the wait, ready to act at a moment's notice.

This concept of patience finds a strong parallel in business, especially in long-term planning and execution. Like a sniper, business leaders often need to wait for the right moment to launch a new product, enter a market, or make a strategic move. This waiting is not passive; it involves actively monitoring the environment, understanding market trends, and preparing for the opportune moment to act. It's a delicate balance between being ready to seize an opportunity and having the patience to wait.

Developing patience in business leadership is akin to a sniper's disciplined waiting. It starts with clearly understanding the goals and recognizing that worthwhile results often take time. This mindset helps manage the natural urge to rush decisions or force outcomes. Business leaders, like snipers, need to trust the process, knowing that their preparation and strategic planning will pay off in due time.

Another strategy is to focus on incremental progress. Just as a sniper remains alert and engaged during their wait, business leaders should focus on making small, continuous improvements. This approach keeps the team motivated and moving forward, even when the larger goal seems distant.

Furthermore, patience in leadership is also about resilience and adaptability. Sometimes, plans need to be adjusted, or unexpected challenges arise. In these moments, the patience to reassess and adapt becomes crucial. It's about maintaining a steady course, even when immediate results are not visible, much like a sniper who must remain focused and ready to adapt their position or strategy as the situation evolves.

In essence, patience and perseverance in sniping and business are about understanding the value of timing, maintaining focus on the long-term vision, and committing to a strategy even when immediate results are not apparent. Cultivating these qualities can lead to more thoughtful decision-making, better-prepared teams, and greater success in achieving long-term objectives.

DECISION-MAKING UNDER PRESSURE

In the life of a sniper, the ability to make quick, accurate decisions under intense pressure is a defining characteristic. These decisions often come in high-stakes situations where a single shot can alter the course of an operation. For a sniper, this means evaluating numerous factors rapidly—wind speed, distance, target movement, and more—all while maintaining composure. The pressure is immense, but their training prepares them to handle it calmly and precisely.

This kind of high-pressure decision-making is not exclusive to the battlefield; it's also a critical aspect of business leadership. In the corporate world, leaders frequently face situations that require swift and decisive action, especially during crises. Whether it's responding to a market downturn, a public relations issue, or an internal crisis, the ability to make clear-headed decisions under pressure is vital.

So, how can one manage and even thrive under such pressure? The techniques used by snipers can be adapted to business scenarios. One key technique is the practice of scenario planning. Snipers train extensively in various scenarios, preparing them to react effectively under different circumstances. Similarly, business leaders can engage in scenario planning, envisioning multiple crisis situations, and developing response strategies. This preparation enables leaders to act more confidently and decisively when a real crisis hits.

Another technique is maintaining situational awareness. Snipers are highly aware of their surroundings and any changes in their environment. In business, this translates to having a

JASON MILLER

deep understanding of the market, competitors, and internal dynamics. Being well-informed allows leaders to make more accurate assessments and better decisions under pressure.

Mindfulness and stress management also play a crucial role. Just as snipers use breathing techniques and mental conditioning to stay calm, business leaders can benefit from stress-reduction practices like meditation, exercise, or even simply taking a moment to breathe and center themselves before making a big decision.

The application of these techniques becomes particularly evident in crisis management. In such situations, leaders must assess the issue quickly, consider the potential impact on the company, and decide on a course of action. This process is akin to a sniper analyzing their target and environment before taking a shot. It requires clarity, calmness, and precision—qualities honed through practice and a deep understanding of the principles of decision-making under pressure.

In conclusion, the ability to make sound decisions under pressure is a skill that can be developed and refined, much like a sniper sharpens their abilities. By adopting some of these sniper techniques, business leaders can enhance their decision-making skills, especially in high-pressure situations, leading to more effective management and better outcomes for their organizations.

RISK ASSESSMENT AND MANAGEMENT

In a sniper's disciplined and dangerous world, assessing and managing risks is a critical aspect of every mission. A sniper must constantly evaluate potential threats and outcomes, considering factors such as visibility, enemy positioning, and escape routes. This constant analysis is crucial for their survival and the success of their mission. They must weigh the risk of

9

taking a shot against the potential reward, always mindful of the broader objectives at stake.

This careful risk assessment and management process has clear parallels in the business world. Business leaders, much like snipers, must navigate a landscape filled with risks, from financial uncertainties to market competition and operational challenges. Effective risk management in business involves identifying potential risks, evaluating their likelihood and impact, and developing mitigation strategies.

One can draw inspiration from sniper training for business risk management strategies. Snipers are trained to anticipate and plan for various scenarios, always having a contingency plan in place. In business, this translates to scenario planning and having backup strategies. Companies that effectively manage risk often have robust plans for potential problems, ensuring they can react quickly and effectively to minimize damage.

To illustrate effective risk management in business, consider the case of a technology company facing the risk of cybersecurity threats. This company, recognizing the potential danger, conducts a thorough risk assessment, identifying vulnerabilities in their systems. They then implement robust security measures like a sniper would secure their position. Additionally, they develop an incident response plan, similar to a sniper's contingency plan, to ensure they can quickly and effectively respond to any breaches.

Another example can be seen in the financial sector, where risk management is an integral part of operations. Financial institutions regularly assess the risk of investments, much like a sniper evaluates their targets. They use sophisticated models to predict market changes and adjust their strategies accordingly. This proactive approach to risk management enables them to navigate market volatility and make informed investment decisions.

In both these cases, the key to successful risk management lies in thorough assessment, careful planning, and adapting to changing circumstances. Just as snipers must constantly reassess their situation and adjust their approach, businesses must remain agile and responsive to emerging risks. By adopting a sniper-like focus on risk assessment and management, businesses can better navigate the uncertainties of the corporate world and achieve their objectives with greater security and confidence.

The Importance of Continuous Training and Adaptation

In the life of an army sniper, continuous training and adaptation are not just part of the job; they are essential for survival and success. An ongoing process of learning and evolving characterizes a sniper's career. This relentless pursuit of improvement ensures they remain effective and prepared for any challenge. Snipers regularly update their skills, learning new techniques and adapting to new technologies and environments. This constant evolution is critical in a field where stagnation can have dire consequences.

This concept of perpetual growth and adaptation is equally vital in business leadership. Leaders cannot afford to remain static in the fast-paced and ever-changing business landscape. Ongoing learning and adaptation are paramount to stay ahead of market trends, technological advancements, and evolving customer needs. Business leaders, much like snipers, must continually sharpen their skills and knowledge to lead their organizations effectively.

Incorporating continuous learning into a business strategy requires a proactive approach. One method is to foster a culture of learning within the organization. This can be achieved by encouraging employee development through workshops, seminars, and training programs. By investing in the growth of their team, leaders not only enhance the capabilities of their workforce but also demonstrate a commitment to the collective advancement of the organization.

Another method is for leaders to engage in personal development actively. This could involve pursuing further education, attending industry conferences, or staying updated with the latest business literature. By dedicating time to their development, leaders can set a powerful example for their teams and bring fresh perspectives and ideas to their organization.

Furthermore, adaptation in business leadership also involves being open to new ideas and approaches. This can mean experimenting with innovative business models, embracing new technologies, or adapting to cultural shifts within the workplace. It's about being flexible and responsive to change, like a sniper who must adapt quickly to a changing battlefield.

In conclusion, continuous training and adaptation are crucial for both snipers and business leaders. The landscape constantly evolves in both fields, and success depends on the ability to learn, grow, and adapt. By embracing a mindset of continuous improvement and staying agile in the face of change, business leaders can navigate the complexities of the corporate world and lead their organizations to sustained success.

ETHICAL CONSIDERATIONS AND RESPONSIBILITY

In the world of a sniper, every decision carries significant ethical weight. The choice to take a shot is not just tactical;

it's steeped in moral considerations. Snipers operate within strict rules of engagement and are constantly aware of the responsibility that comes with their role. Their decisions can have far-reaching implications, affecting their targets and the broader context of their missions. This deep sense of ethical responsibility is critical to their profession, guiding their actions and decisions.

Though different in context, the business realm is similarly laden with ethical considerations. Business leaders are often faced with decisions that test their moral compass. From financial dealings to employee relations and environmental practices, every choice can significantly impact the company, stakeholders, and society at large. Ethical decision-making in business is not just about complying with laws and regulations; it's about upholding values and principles that guide the company's conduct.

Let's look at a few case studies to understand how ethical considerations play out in the business world. One notable example is a technology firm prioritizing user privacy in its product development. Despite the potential for higher profits through data monetization, the company's leadership upheld strict privacy standards, earning customer trust and loyalty. This decision, grounded in ethical principles, not only reinforced their brand's integrity but also set a precedent for responsible data management in the industry.

Another case is a clothing manufacturer who faced the challenge of ensuring fair labor practices in their overseas factories. The company's leaders took proactive steps to audit their supply chain, implement fair wages, and improve working conditions. This commitment to ethical labor practices enhanced their reputation and attracted a customer base that values social responsibility.

These examples illustrate how ethical leadership and corporate responsibility can shape a company's identity and influence its success. Just as a sniper must consider the ethical dimensions of their decisions, business leaders must navigate complex moral landscapes, making choices that reflect their values and principles. Ethical decision-making requires courage and integrity, but it can lead to a business that thrives financially and contributes positively to society.

In conclusion, ethical considerations and responsibility are fundamental both in a sniper's life and in the business world. They are the pillars upon which trust and credibility are built. For business leaders, embracing ethical decision-making and corporate responsibility is not just a legal obligation; it's a commitment to doing what's right, fostering a culture of integrity, and building a legacy of positive impact.

BRINGING IT ALL TOGETHER: A SNIPER'S APPROACH TO BUSINESS LEADERSHIP

As we conclude our exploration into the disciplined world of a sniper and its application to business leadership, it's clear that the parallels between the two are profound and instructive. The life of a sniper, characterized by precision, focus, patience, decision-making under pressure, risk assessment, continuous adaptation, and ethical responsibility, offers a wealth of lessons for anyone aspiring to lead in the business arena.

Snipers are masters of precision, calculating every detail of their mission meticulously. When applied to business, this level of precision translates to strategic planning, execution, and measurement. It's about aligning resources and efforts towards clearly defined goals and ensuring that every action is intentional and well-considered.

The unparalleled focus of a sniper, their ability to maintain concentration amidst distractions and maintain mental clarity under pressure, is a skill of immense value in the fast-paced world of business. This focus enables business leaders to navigate complex projects, make strategic decisions, and lead their teams effectively through challenges.

Patience and perseverance, so central to a sniper's routine, are equally important in business, especially in long-term planning and execution. Leaders must learn the art of waiting for the right moment to act, maintaining a steady course toward their objectives, even when immediate results are not evident.

The ability to make decisions under pressure is a hallmark of both snipers and successful business leaders. In high-stakes situations, leaders must remain calm, assess the situation quickly, and make informed, strategic decisions that could have significant implications for their organizations.

Risk assessment and management, a vital aspect of a sniper's mission, offers a template for business leaders to identify, evaluate, and mitigate potential threats. This proactive approach to risk management is crucial for navigating the uncertainties of the business world.

Continuous training and adaptation, as exemplified by snipers, highlight the importance of lifelong learning and flexibility in leadership. In a world where change is the only constant, leaders must remain open to new ideas, continuously develop their skills, and adapt their strategies to stay relevant and practical.

Finally, the ethical dimensions governing a sniper's decisions are a powerful lesson in corporate responsibility and ethical leadership. Business leaders must navigate complex moral landscapes, make choices that reflect their values and principles, and contribute positively to society.

Adopting a sniper's approach to business leadership—characterized by precision, focus, patience, decision-making under pressure, risk management, continuous learning, and ethical responsibility—can create a disciplined, focused, and successful leader. These qualities, honed in the demanding environment of military service, offer a blueprint for excellence in the corporate world, guiding leaders to make strategic decisions, lead effectively, and achieve lasting success.

As we conclude our journey through the parallels between the discipline of a sniper and the qualities of effective business leadership, it's important to reflect on the key insights we've gleaned. This exploration has revealed that the principles guiding a sniper—precision, focus, patience, decision-making under pressure, risk management, continuous learning, and ethical responsibility—are relevant and invaluable in business leadership.

We've seen how the sniper's hallmark of precision mirrors the need for strategic clarity and meticulous execution in business. Precision in planning and action ensures that resources are used effectively, and goals are accurately met. Focus, a critical skill for a sniper, is equally essential in the corporate world, where leaders must navigate a maze of distractions and maintain clarity of purpose.

Patience and perseverance, so integral to a sniper's success, teach us the value of waiting for the right moment in business and the importance of resilience in the face of challenges. The ability to make decisions under intense pressure, a skill honed by snipers, is vital for business leaders who often face high-stakes situations requiring swift and decisive action.

Risk assessment and management, a constant in a sniper's world, offers a model for identifying and mitigating potential threats in business, ensuring that companies can confidently navigate uncertainties. The emphasis on continuous training and adaptation in a sniper's career underscores the importance of lifelong learning and flexibility in leadership, which are essential for staying ahead in a rapidly changing business environment.

Lastly, the ethical considerations governing a sniper's actions are a powerful lesson in corporate responsibility and moral leadership. In business, making decisions that are not only profitable but also ethical and socially responsible is crucial for long-term success and sustainability.

As we wrap up this chapter, the message is clear: the discipline and skills of a sniper are not just relevant for the battlefield; they are crucial for business leadership. By adopting these principles, business leaders can enhance their decision-making abilities, refine their strategies, and lead their organizations to greater heights. Whether you're at the helm of a small startup or a large corporation, these lessons offer a blueprint for effective leadership, strategic success, and a legacy of positive impact. Let's embrace these qualities and move forward with the confidence and precision of a sniper, aiming not just for immediate success but for enduring excellence in the business.

ACTION STEPS

1. **Implement Precision in Your Strategic Planning**: Just as a sniper meticulously plans every detail of their mission, apply this level of precision to your business strategy. This means carefully analyzing market trends, understanding customer needs, and aligning your resources effectively. Start by conducting a thorough review of your business objectives and operational processes. Identify areas lacking precision and develop a detailed plan to address these gaps. This could involve

refining your marketing strategy, optimizing your supply chain, or enhancing product quality. The goal is to ensure that every aspect of your business is aligned and functioning with sniper-like precision.

2. **Cultivate a Culture of Continuous Learning and Adaptation**: Inspired by the sniper's commitment to ongoing training and adaptability, prioritize continuous learning within your organization. Encourage your team to embrace new challenges and learn new skills. This could be facilitated through regular training sessions, workshops, or even encouraging self-led learning and development. Additionally, stay abreast of industry trends and technological advancements and be willing to adapt your business practices accordingly. This approach keeps your business competitive and fosters a dynamic and innovative work environment.

3. **Enhance Decision-Making Under Pressure**: Drawing from the sniper's ability to make critical decisions under high pressure, improve how you handle challenging situations in your business. Start by practicing stress management techniques such as mindfulness or deep breathing, which can help maintain clarity of thought during stressful times. Additionally, develop a structured approach to problem-solving, which includes gathering relevant information, considering various perspectives, and weighing the potential outcomes before making a decision. By enhancing your ability to make composed and informed decisions in high-pressure scenarios, you can confidently navigate business challenges and lead your team.

About the Author

Jason Miller is an accomplished business leader with over thirty years of experience, renowned for his expertise in hyper company growth, scaling, and strategic and operational implementation. He founded the Strategic Advisor Board (SAB) in 2017 and served as its Senior Global Council Member, overseeing its global operations and team capabilities. In addition to his primary role at SAB, Jason holds multiple chair positions across various companies and nonprofits. He has built more than twenty-four companies from scratch since 2001 and is dedicated to crafting sustainable business models emphasizing leadership responsibility, strategy, and accountability.

Known for his no-excuses approach and nicknamed "The Bull," Jason has advised thousands of global leaders. He has been recognized as a foremost expert in consulting for creating scalable business models, particularly for small and mid-market companies. His focus extends to fostering a positive company culture, enhancing staff retention, and deepening customer loyalty, believing that a clear vision and purpose are essential for impactful business. As a veteran, Jason is committed to serving veteran-owned companies and provides pro bono services to veteran organizations as part of a five-year plan.

Jason holds an MBA from Trident University and credits the "school of hard knocks" for his doctorate in practical experience. He is affiliated with numerous prestigious organizations that impact business globally, such as the American Club Association, Leigh Steinberg Academy, Forbes Council, and Entrepreneur Magazine Leadership Council. A lifetime member of the American Legion, Disabled American Veterans, and Veterans of Foreign Wars, Jason lives in Boulder, Colorado, with his family. He focuses on professional development and business strategy to serve his clients better.

THE ANTIFRAGILE MINDSET: A CEO'S DAILY PRACTICE

CHRIS O'BYRNE

The antifragile mindset is a distinctive approach to business and life. It's about gaining from disorder. Unlike being resilient or robust, which suggests withstanding shocks, antifragility means improving when exposed to volatility and stress. It's a concept that takes setbacks and turns them into a driving force for growth. In business, this mindset isn't just beneficial; it's essential for thriving in an environment where change is the only constant.

Leadership demands more than just guiding a team or making decisions. In the realm of antifragility, it's about leading in a way that not only withstands challenges but also uses them as fuel for improvement and innovation. This approach is crucial in today's fast-paced business environment. An anti-fragile leader doesn't just endure hardships; they leverage these experiences to strengthen their team, refine their strategies, and advance their organization.

But how does one develop an antifragile mindset? It's a journey, not a destination. It involves a daily commitment to growth and adaptability. Each day is an opportunity to reinforce this mindset through decision-making, risk management, and strategic planning. For a CEO, fostering antifragility means making choices that encourage adaptability and learning in the face of uncertainty.

Embracing uncertainty is a cornerstone of the antifragile mindset. In business, change and unpredictability are inevitable. Accepting this reality allows me to remain flexible in my strategies and responsive to new challenges. This mindset helps me to not just navigate through tough times but also to spot opportunities where others might see dead ends.

Beyond personal development, cultivating an antifragile mindset involves creating a culture of innovation and resilience within the organization. It's about encouraging the team to embrace change, experiment boldly, and learn from every outcome, whether a success or a failure. As a leader, my goal is to build an environment where continuous improvement is the norm. This culture ensures that the organization survives challenges and thrives on them, growing stronger and more capable with every hurdle we overcome.

THE ORIGIN OF "ANTIFRAGILITY"

The concept of "antifragility" was introduced and popularized by Nassim Nicholas Taleb in his book *Antifragile: Things That Gain from Disorder*, published in 2012. Taleb, an essayist, scholar, statistician, former trader, and risk analyst, is known for his work focusing on problems of randomness, probability, and uncertainty.

Taleb's concept of antifragility goes beyond the traditional understanding of resilience or robustness. While something resilient resists shocks and stays the same, something antifragile improves when exposed to volatility, randomness, disorder, and stressors. Taleb argues that in complex systems, like economic and political systems, attempts to suppress volatility can make these systems more vulnerable to catastrophic failure. In contrast, allowing systems to experience stressors can strengthen them as they adapt and improve in response to challenges.

The antifragile concept has its roots in Taleb's earlier work on randomness and uncertainty, particularly the idea of "black swan events" — unpredictable and rare events with extreme impacts, which he discussed in his 2007 book *The Black Swan*. With *Antifragile*, Taleb extended these ideas, suggesting that systems should be able to withstand unpredictable shocks and can be designed in such a way that they benefit from them.

Taleb's antifragile theory has influenced various fields, including economics, finance, management, engineering, and personal development. It has inspired individuals and organizations to adopt strategies that are not just about survival in the face of adversity but about using volatility and challenges as opportunities for growth and improvement. This approach has profound implications for how people manage risk, make decisions, and plan for the future in a world of uncertainty and rapid change.

Understanding Antifragility

Understanding antifragility begins with differentiating it from resilience. While resilience is about bouncing back from setbacks, antifragility goes a step further. It's about growing more robust in the face of adversity. In business, this distinction is critical. A resilient leader might recover from a crisis, but an antifragile leader uses that crisis to improve their strategies and decision-making processes. This mindset turns challenges into opportunities for growth and innovation.

The role of stressors and challenges in fostering antifragile growth is pivotal. In my experience, these are not just obstacles to overcome but essential for development. When faced with stressors, whether market fluctuations, competitive pressures, or internal challenges, an antifragile mindset sees these as chances to learn and adapt. This perspective transforms potential negatives into positives, driving personal and organizational growth.

Embracing uncertainty and volatility is at the heart of antifragility. In business, change is constant and often unpredictable. Instead of fearing this uncertainty, I've learned to welcome it. This approach has not only helped me navigate through complex situations but has also allowed me to identify and seize opportunities that others might miss. By accepting that change is inevitable, I've become more adaptable and agile, qualities that are indispensable in today's business environment.

Developing an antifragile mindset requires a shift in perspective. It's about viewing every challenge as a chance to improve, no matter how daunting. This approach has been a game-changer for me. It has allowed me to turn potential crises into growth catalysts for myself and my business. This mindset doesn't eliminate challenges, but it changes how I respond to them, ensuring that each one contributes to my development and the success of my organization.

In conclusion, antifragility is more than just a concept; it's a practical approach to business and leadership. It involves recognizing the difference between resilience and antifragility, understanding the role of stressors and challenges, and embracing uncertainty and volatility. By adopting this mindset, I've become a more effective leader and guided my business to new heights, turning potential setbacks into stepping stones for success.

CULTIVATING AN ANTIFRAGILE MINDSET

Cultivating an antifragile mindset begins with mindfulness and self-awareness. In my role as a leader in business, this has meant consistently taking time to reflect on my actions, decisions, and their outcomes. Mindfulness helps me stay grounded and aware of the present moment, enabling me to respond to situations with clarity and purpose. On the other hand, self-awareness allows me to understand my strengths and weaknesses, making me more open to growth and development. This combination of mindfulness and self-awareness is a powerful tool in building an antifragile mindset, as it keeps me connected to my core values while navigating the complexities of business.

Continuous learning and adaptability are also crucial components of an antifragile mindset. The business world is dynamic, with new challenges and opportunities emerging regularly. To stay ahead, I've learned to embrace a mindset of continuous learning. This means staying curious, seeking new knowledge, and being willing to adapt my strategies in response to new information. Adaptability has been particularly valuable, allowing me to pivot when necessary and find innovative solutions to the challenges that arise. By committing to lifelong learning and flexibility, I've been able to grow not just as a leader but also guide my business through various stages of evolution.

Embracing risk and learning from failure are perhaps the most challenging yet rewarding aspects of cultivating an antifragile mindset. In business, taking risks is often necessary for growth and innovation. However, with risk comes the possibility of failure. Instead of fearing failure, I've learned to embrace it as an integral part of learning. Each failure provides valuable lessons and insights that can be used to improve future strategies. This approach has made me more resilient and fostered a culture of innovation within my organization, where taking calculated risks is seen as a pathway to success.

In my experience, the journey to developing an antifragile mindset is ongoing. It requires a commitment to self-improvement, a willingness to adapt, and the courage to embrace risks and learn from failures. This mindset has helped me become a better leader and has also been instrumental in guiding my business through uncertain times. By staying mindful, continually learning, and embracing both risk and failure, I've turned challenges into opportunities for growth, making my business more robust and resilient.

Developing an antifragile mindset is not about eliminating challenges or avoiding risks. It's about transforming the way we perceive and respond to these factors. By cultivating mindfulness, embracing continuous learning, and learning from successes and failures, we can build a resilient business that thrives on the challenges that might otherwise have been setbacks. This mindset is a powerful tool for navigating the business and leading with confidence and foresight.

DAILY PRACTICES FOR ANTIFRAGILE THINKING

Starting each day with reflective journaling has become a cornerstone of my routine as a leader in business. This practice goes beyond merely recording events; it's a structured method for processing my thoughts and experiences. Each morning, I reflect on the previous day's challenges and successes. This process allows me to clarify my goals and the steps needed to achieve them. Journaling fosters a deeper understanding of my actions and decisions, enabling me to identify areas for improvement and reinforcing my antifragile mindset.

Setting dynamic goals and priorities is another daily practice that bolsters my antifragile thinking. In the ever-evolving world of business, static goals can quickly become obsolete. Therefore, I ensure that my goals are flexible and adaptable to change. This approach involves regularly assessing and adjusting my objectives in response to new information and changing circumstances. By setting dynamic goals, I can stay aligned with my long-term vision and be nimble enough to navigate the unpredictability that characterizes today's business environment.

Encouraging open communication and establishing feedback loops within my team is crucial for maintaining an antifragile mindset. I firmly believe that diverse perspectives and collaborative problem-solving lead to more robust and innovative solutions. Therefore, I foster an environment where team members feel valued and heard. Regular meetings and open forums for sharing ideas and feedback are part of our routine. This openness enhances team cohesion and contributes to a collective antifragile mindset, where challenges are approached with a shared sense of purpose and adaptability.

In my daily operations, I prioritize these practices to cultivate an antifragile mindset, both personally and within my organization. Reflective journaling helps maintain a clear and focused mind, setting dynamic goals ensures agility in planning, and encouraging open communication fosters a collaborative and resilient team environment. These practices are integral to developing a business that survives and thrives in the face of challenges and uncertainties.

Adopting these daily practices has profoundly impacted my approach to business and leadership. The discipline of reflective journaling, the adaptability in goal setting, and the collaborative strength of open communication have become the pillars of my leadership style. They have enabled me to create a business culture that is not just resilient but truly antifragile, capable of using challenges as opportunities for growth and innovation. This approach has enhanced my effectiveness as a leader and guided my team in navigating and succeeding in the dynamic and often unpredictable world of business.

BUILDING ANTIFRAGILE TEAMS AND CULTURES

Building antifragile teams and cultures within my organization starts with fostering a culture of innovation and experimentation. In my role, I emphasize the value of exploring new ideas and encourage my team to think outside the box. This environment allows for a free flow of creativity, where unique solutions are born from challenges. By promoting experimentation, I aim to create a workspace where failure is not feared but seen as a necessary step towards discovery and innovation. This approach has led to significant breakthroughs in our projects and ingrained a sense of daring and inventiveness in our team culture.

Encouraging team resilience and adaptability is another critical aspect of building an antifragile culture. In the fast-paced environment of business, adaptability is crucial. I consistently work with my team to develop skills that enhance their ability to adjust to new situations and challenges. This involves training, workshops, and regular team discussions on building resilience. We learn to anticipate changes, adapt our strategies, and remain flexible. This resilience helps us navigate difficult times and positions us to capitalize on new opportunities as they arise.

Leading by example is vital in demonstrating antifragile behaviors. I understand that my actions and attitudes as a leader set the tone for the entire team. Therefore, I try to model antifragility in my daily interactions and decisions. This includes showing openness to new ideas, willingness to adapt, and maintaining a positive outlook despite setbacks. By doing so,

I aim to inspire my team to adopt similar behaviors, creating a collective strength greater than the sum of its parts.

In my experience, the journey to building an antifragile team and culture is ongoing. It requires consistent effort and a commitment to fostering an environment that values innovation, resilience, and adaptability. As we continue to grow and face new challenges, these qualities become more deeply ingrained in our team's ethos, enhancing our capacity to thrive in an ever-changing business environment.

I have witnessed a remarkable transformation in my team by fostering innovation, encouraging resilience, and leading by example. We have evolved into a unit that withstands pressures and uncertainties and uses them as catalysts for growth and success. This shift towards an antifragile culture has enhanced our performance and made our work environment more dynamic, fulfilling, and prepared to tackle future business challenges.

DECISION-MAKING AND PROBLEM-SOLVING

Integrating antifragile principles into decision-making has reshaped how I approach problems in business. Every decision now goes through a filter of antifragility. This means I constantly ask myself: Will this choice strengthen my organization in the face of future challenges? This approach has led me to favor decisions that not only solve immediate problems but also build resilience and adaptability into the fabric of my organization. It's about looking beyond the quick fix to choices that offer long-term benefits, even if they require more effort or resources in the short term.

Navigating complex challenges with antifragile strategies involves a shift in mindset. When faced with a difficult situation, my first step is not to seek a way around the problem but through it. I look for strategies that will not only address the issue at hand but also prepare us for similar challenges in the future. This might mean choosing a more challenging path that offers greater learning and growth opportunities. By tackling problems this way, my team and I often discover innovative solutions that we might not have considered if we were only looking for the easiest way out.

Balancing short-term adaptability with a long-term vision is a delicate act but essential in antifragile decision-making. While it's important to remain flexible and responsive to immediate challenges, losing sight of the long-term vision can lead to a reactive rather than a strategic approach. To maintain this balance, I regularly revisit our long-term goals to ensure our short-term actions are aligned with them. This helps us make decisions that are adaptable in the short run and contribute to our long-term objectives.

In my role, decision-making is about choosing the right path and preparing the organization for future uncertainties. Integrating antifragile principles means that each decision is an opportunity to strengthen the organization. Whether it's a minor operational choice or a major strategic move, the focus is always on building a more resilient and adaptable business.

Adopting antifragile strategies in decision-making and problem-solving has been transformative for my business. It has led to a culture where challenges are welcomed as opportunities for growth. This approach has made us more innovative and resilient and ensured that our business is well-positioned to thrive in an ever-changing environment. By focusing on long-term vision while adapting to short-term realities, we strike a balance that drives our success and prepares us for whatever the future holds.

MAINTAINING BALANCE AND WELLNESS

Maintaining balance and wellness is crucial in cultivating an antifragile mindset, especially in the demanding world of business. For me, physical and mental well-being are not just personal priorities but essential foundations for professional effectiveness. Regular exercise, a balanced diet, and adequate rest are non-negotiable aspects of my routine. They keep me physically robust and mentally sharp, enabling me to handle the stresses and strains of my role with resilience. Similarly, mental wellness practices like meditation and mindfulness help me maintain clarity and focus, which are crucial for making sound decisions and leading effectively.

Balancing work and personal life is another vital aspect of maintaining overall well-being. The nature of my work often blurs the lines between professional and personal time. I set clear boundaries to combat this and prioritize time with family and engaging in hobbies. This separation is essential for personal happiness and maintaining a fresh perspective and energy in my professional life. Taking time off from work is not a luxury; it's a necessity that helps recharge my batteries and fuels my productivity when I return to the office.

Developing emotional intelligence and empathy has been transformative for my leadership style. Understanding and managing my own emotions is key to interacting effectively with others. It allows me to respond rather than react in challenging situations. Empathy, the ability to understand and share the feelings of others, has improved my relationships with team members, leading to a more cohesive and supportive work environment. These skills are not innate; they require continuous cultivation through self-reflection, feedback from others, and a genuine interest in the well-being of those around me.

In my journey as a leader, I have learned that neglecting personal well-being can undermine even the most effective business strategies. Physical health, mental clarity, emotional intelligence, and a balanced lifestyle are not just personal benefits; they are the bedrock upon which sustainable professional success is built. I am better equipped to handle my business and lead my team effectively by taking care of myself.

This holistic approach to wellness has proven to be a key component of an antifragile mindset. By maintaining physical health, mental clarity, work-life balance, and emotional intelligence, I've built a strong foundation that supports my personal growth and the growth and resilience of my business. It's a continuous process of self-improvement that contributes significantly to both personal fulfillment and professional achievement.

CASE STUDIES AND REAL-WORLD EXAMPLES

In my career, I have encountered several leaders who exemplify the antifragile mindset. One such leader was the CEO of a tech startup I worked with. Faced with the sudden departure of an investor, she transformed what could have been a crippling setback into a catalyst for change. Instead of seeking immediate financial rescue, she restructured the company's operations, diversifying revenue streams and reducing dependency on external funding. This stabilized the company and attracted new investors impressed by its resilience. Her approach demonstrated how antifragile leaders use crises to strengthen their organizations.

Another instance where I witnessed antifragility in action was in a manufacturing company during an economic downturn. While competitors were downsizing, this company used the opportunity to invest in employee training and process improvements. They emerged from the downturn with a more skilled workforce and efficient operations, gaining a significant market share. This company's forward-thinking approach during tough times was a practical application of antifragility – using adversity as an opportunity for growth.

Antifragile businesses often share traits such as adaptability, innovation, and a culture that embraces challenges. A retail chain I collaborated with exemplified this. When faced with the rise of e-commerce, instead of viewing it as a threat, they integrated it into their business model. They used their physical stores for unique customer experiences while enhancing their online presence. This dual approach turned a potential challenge into a thriving business opportunity, showcasing the power of an antifragile strategy.

In various industries, the principles of antifragility manifest differently but with a common theme: turning challenges into opportunities. In healthcare, for instance, a hospital I worked with used patient feedback, which was initially negative, to overhaul its service delivery. This improved patient care and positioned the hospital as a leader in patient satisfaction. Similarly, schools facing declining enrollment in education due to online learning options innovated their curriculum and teaching methods, attracting a new demographic of students.

These real-world examples underscore the versatility and effectiveness of the antifragile approach. Whether in tech startups, manufacturing, retail, healthcare, or education, leaders who embrace antifragility navigate their organizations through challenges and use these situations to emerge more robust and competitive. The lessons learned from these cases are clear: in the face of adversity, the antifragile mindset is not just about survival; it's about leveraging challenges for transformation and growth.

DAILY REFLECTION AND CONTINUOUS IMPROVEMENT

Daily reflection has become essential to my routine, significantly contributing to my antifragile growth. I set aside time each evening to review the day's events, decisions, and outcomes. This isn't just a casual recap; it's a deliberate process to extract lessons and insights. Reflecting on both successes and setbacks helps me understand what worked and what didn't. During these moments of contemplation, I often identify new opportunities for growth and improvement. This practice keeps me grounded and focused, ensuring that each day contributes to my development as an antifragile leader.

Continuous improvement and learning are at the core of an antifragile mindset. I view my professional journey as an ongoing cycle of learning, applying, and evolving. This cycle begins with acquiring new knowledge or skills, which I then use in practical scenarios. These applications' outcomes, whether successes or failures, become new learning opportunities. This cycle of continuous improvement helps me stay adaptable and forward-thinking. It's an approach that keeps me and my business evolving, ensuring we are always prepared to meet new challenges and exploit new opportunities.

Learning cycles in an antifragile context are not just about personal growth; they extend to my team and the entire organization. I encourage my team members to engage in their own cycles of learning and improvement. We share our experiences and insights, creating a collective pool of knowledge that benefits the entire organization. This shared learning culture fosters unity and purpose, continually driving us to improve and adapt as a cohesive unit.

Setting the stage for tomorrow's antifragile practice is about applying today's reflections and learnings to future actions. After my daily reflection, I plan to use the insights gained the next day. This might mean adjusting strategies, experimenting with new approaches, or continuing practices that proved effective. This forward-looking approach ensures that each day builds upon the last, creating a momentum of growth and antifragility.

Daily reflection and continuous improvement have become integral to my leadership and the culture of my organization. This approach has helped me develop a more robust and adaptable mindset and positioned my business to thrive amidst change and uncertainty. By focusing on reflection, learning, and application, we set a solid foundation for continuous antifragile growth, ready to embrace whatever challenges and opportunities the future holds.

Reflecting on the principles of an antifragile mindset, it's clear that this approach has profoundly influenced my leadership and business practices. The key lies in embracing challenges as opportunities for growth rather than mere obstacles. This mindset has taught me the importance of resilience, surviving difficult times, and using these experiences to emerge stronger and more adept. It's about seeing the potential for improvement in every setback and viewing uncertainty not as a threat but as a playground for innovation.

The journey of antifragile leadership is ongoing, filled with constant learning and adaptation. It's a path that requires courage to face the unknown and the humility to learn from every experience, whether good or bad. As a leader, I have found that fostering an antifragile mindset is not a one-time task but a continuous endeavor. It involves daily practices like reflection, embracing change, and seeking out challenges as catalysts for growth.

For fellow CEOs and leaders, my encouragement is to embrace the principles of antifragility in your own leadership styles.

It's a transformative approach that can significantly impact your personal development and the success of your business. Remember, antifragility is not about avoiding failure; it's about using every experience, every challenge, and every failure as a tool for growth.

As leaders, we have the unique opportunity to apply these principles to our lives and instill them in our organizations. By cultivating a culture that embraces learning, adaptation, and resilience, we can build teams and businesses that are not just capable of surviving in a dynamic environment but are poised to thrive and innovate.

Embracing antifragility is about more than just personal or organizational success; it's about setting a standard for leadership that is dynamic, robust, and ever-evolving. It's a commitment to growth, learning, and resilience that can redefine our approach to challenges and change. As we continue on this journey, let's remember that the essence of antifragile leadership lies in using adversity as a springboard for growth and innovation, setting the stage for a future that is as resilient as it is bright.

ACTION STEPS

1. **Embrace Challenges as Opportunities**: After reading the chapter, you can start viewing challenges as hurdles to overcome and opportunities for growth and innovation. When faced with a difficult situation in your business, instead of immediately seeking a workaround, consider how this challenge can be leveraged to improve your business practices, develop new strategies, or enhance your team's skills. This shift in mindset can transform potential setbacks into catalysts for advancement.

2. **Cultivate a Culture of Continuous Learning**: The author's insights encourage the development of a learning-oriented environment within your business. You can encourage your team to engage in continuous learning and experimentation. This involves personal development and motivating your team to share insights and experiences. Establishing a culture where learning from successes and failures is valued can lead to a more adaptable and innovative business.

3. **Implement Daily Reflection and Adaptive Planning**: Incorporate the practice of daily reflection into your routine, as suggested by the author. Take time each day to assess your decisions, strategies, and their outcomes. Use these reflections to adapt your plans. This can help you remain agile in your decision-making process and ensure that your business strategies stay aligned with changing circumstances and long-term goals. By consistently applying these insights, you can foster an antifragile approach to business, enabling your organization to thrive amidst uncertainty.

ABOUT THE AUTHOR

Chris O'Byrne is the CEO of Jetlaunch Publishing and has published over 15,000 books in seventeen years. He has published books for authors such as John Lee Dumas, Ed Mylett, Rachel Pedersen, Joe Vitale, and Kary Oberbrunner. He has created over one hundred partnerships and has 15 international bestsellers to his name. He is the editor-in-chief of the influential business magazine, Pivot Magazine, which reaches millions in distribution and has featured such people as Robert Kiyosaki, General Petreaus (former director of the CIA), and Joe Foster, founder of Reebok.

THE TEST OF DISCIPLINE

TONY D'URSO

During my most recent transition to a new business venture, I encountered a heavily regulated industry, much like the disruptions of 2020 to 2021. Everything changed. I had to adapt swiftly, establish a successful business, and accelerate onto the freeway as quickly as possible. This predated the madness of 2020 when other similar events happened. Despite my extensive corporate experience, I faced numerous challenges, notably the shift from discipline to consistent execution.

I experimented with various available programs, each with its own set of issues. Some were too cumbersome, while others demanded constant visibility. Some operated in the background, disappeared when needed, or took up too much computing power, necessitating shutdown while multitasking. Some inundated you with too much paperwork, undermining efficiency. Additionally, when a computer crashed, the application often got wiped out, resulting in a restart. My experience with those older applications led me to seek better alternatives. As for the newer, current applications, I can't provide insights since I've since transitioned away from them.

Despite the challenges encountered with the best and brightest solutions available at the time, as each had issues, I resorted to the age-old favorite and improved upon it. I grabbed a legal pad and pen, drew a line down the middle, and jotted down the crucial tasks that aligned with my master plan, tactical steps, and overall vision. I concisely described what needed to be accomplished—one item, one task. This final step marked the fulfillment of my developed vision map, consisting of eight essential steps.

The last step becomes part of your to-do list, which is incredibly portable. It doesn't rely on electricity or the internet. Whether traveling or facing computer issues, your list remains right by your side on paper. The beauty of this system is that a task stays on that paper until you complete it; you never lose track of what needs to be done. It's a constant reminder, patiently waiting for your attention, ensuring discipline. You progress from one task to the next, whether you work for a few hours or take breaks, as your list is always there, ready to check off tasks.

Before adopting this method, I often pondered what to do next, especially when starting my workday. I'm sure you've been in that situation, too, wondering about your top priorities. How much time have you wasted deciding what's most important, and how many essential tasks have you forgotten? How much time do you spend figuring out what to do next? This process solves those challenges effectively. The precise set of steps helped my podcast become the number one show on Voice of America and a global leader on Charitable. With these steps, my show has attracted over 40 million listeners in just seven years.

You'll hear this from others, and I agree wholeheartedly: Consistency is everything. It defines you and your company, shaping your brand identity.

With prior experience in corporate marketing, I had a basic grasp of icons and brands. I recognized their significance and had achieved success in that realm. However, my perspective on these matters expanded when I transitioned to podcasting.

Everything matters because everything you present shapes your identity. I'm referring to your images, brand icons, fonts, colors, etc. Consistency is critical. In fact, this subject is so intricate that it warrants a book of its own.

Even if you're an entrepreneur or solopreneur, you will likely have a team, including affiliates, subcontractors, and tech professionals. Although you hire their services, you still serve as a leader in your business, and it's crucial to acknowledge this from the outset.

Maintaining consistency requires substantial time, effort, and continuous communication with my team. Ensuring they grasp this concept hasn't always been straightforward. When you feel like tearing your hair out or getting frustrated, resist the urge. Instead, recognize that patience is a fundamental aspect of achieving unwavering consistency.

You should be patient with your team and consistently communicate your expectations. For example, while writing one of my new books, I requested a specific change to the cover. I asked for it in writing about four times, remaining patient. When I asked the fifth time, it seemed as if the previous requests were forgotten. I mention this as a crucial point because reacting with frustration doesn't lead to progress.

The person didn't quite translate your words into action; there was a disconnect. Patience is key to bridging that gap and ensuring they understand your vision. It's tough, but consistency is vital.

Some tasks take months, and I prefer to persistently request completion rather than hiring someone new, considering the steep learning curve and potential repetition of instructions for a new person. The task, listed in your things to do, remains open and isn't crossed off until it's finished.

This puts you in a situation where you must repeatedly request a step from an employee until it's completed, as it's essential for subsequent tasks. It's like a chain reaction, where each task depends on the previous one. Patience plays an important role in maintaining consistency throughout the process.

When I started podcasting, I managed everything from my domain. When I published a new episode, it would automatically appear on all other podcast platforms. However, after about a year, my domain was hacked. Someone or a group would sporadically delete my site's content, shows, and images. I kept restoring what was lost. However, the security breach persisted, and we engaged in this back-and-forth for several months.

In the end, everything was wiped out, and my podcast disappeared. I found myself at a crossroads, contemplating a return to corporate life or doing something else. This was a source of great despair as I reflected on the initial motivations that led me to podcasting—the desire for something I could manage and work on independently from anywhere in the world. Podcasting offered unparalleled freedom.

I lacked a revenue model during the hacking incident, making it tough to continue podcasting. However, I realized that I had successfully built the podcast once before, and I could do it again. I also had my Vision Map™ to guide me through the necessary steps to relaunch my show, so I worked tirelessly and pushed through the challenges.

As you focus on your key tasks, fatigue, and burnout become less likely since you already have a clear plan. By following your prepared list, you can identify quick-to-complete items. As you check them off, your work becomes more enjoyable and fun. This increased enjoyment boosts your energy, leading you to work diligently and even resent interruptions like ending the workday or going to dinner because you're so immersed in building your empire.

I eventually relaunched my show, resolving the hacking issues. You wouldn't notice any problems as a podcast consumer because I rarely mentioned the issue, except in occasional interviews. I refrained from giving the hacker any satisfaction and pressed on silently.

This highlights a crucial aspect of dealing with failure. Discussing it can inadvertently give it undue attention and significance. Therefore, I chose to remain quiet about it and carried on, eventually creating a better, stronger show that continued to gain a strong following in downloads.

I've mentioned line items on your to-do list in the Vision Map. Let's delve deeper into daily discipline. I maintained a consistent wake-up time each day, a practice I'd longed for in the corporate world when I had to get up at 6:30 a.m. When I started podcasting, the dream of setting my schedule came true. While you might think I get up late every day, it's a reliable routine, with plenty of hours before noon.

My daily routine begins with responding to every single email I have. I look at it like having a conversation with someone; I wouldn't just walk away, and the same applies to emails. Even when faced with a high volume of 100 emails a day and 1,000 monthly interview requests for my weekly show, I make it a point to reply to each one. Without fail, every morning, I address these messages. Any task aligning with my vision and purpose is converted into a to-do list item, meticulously handwritten and retained until completion.

I understand that there's an opposing viewpoint, but consider this, especially when launching a new business and striving for sustainable revenue: When generating income, can you afford to overlook emails from potential prospects or clients? What if opportunities or tasks within them could contribute to increased revenue? I believe you can't ignore messages directed at you. I respond to all emails at the start of the day with full energy and enthusiasm, a critical practice.

Another important step is to avoid eating at your desk, a habit I learned from my corporate experience. Eating at your desk can quickly turn your day into chaos, and I've been through that stressful period in the past. It was the worst time of my life, and I've since sworn off eating at my desk, even at home. The takeaway here is to establish your rules and routines and adhere to them. While your rules and routines may not be ideal for everyone, they work for you, so stick to them for now.

As a former professional typist in corporate America, I've learned the importance of having clean and neatly trimmed fingernails when working at a computer. It's a lesson I picked up through experience because, without this, your fingers can easily slip on the keyboard while typing.

Incorporating a practice I learned during my corporate career, I make it a point to have a sustaining lunch and take a break. When I worked in the office, I used to walk to lunch, and that brief change of environment helped reenergize me for the afternoon. While working from home is different, the principle remains the same. As mentioned earlier, I never eat at my desk. I take short breaks to enjoy a proper meal, then dive back into work, maintaining a high pace until it's time for dinner. Typically, this marks the end of my workday, but there are exceptions depending on the stage of my business and any looming deadlines. For example, I might continue working after dinner if I'm trying to meet a specific show deadline. Otherwise, I call it a day and shift my focus to other activities.

It's worth noting that I didn't mention social media or personal phone calls. I've developed a strict discipline in this regard, influenced by my corporate experiences. I refrain from social chatting until my workday is over. As you might have already guessed, I don't do this in my office, not because I'm being aloof but because I've learned that my desk is where I'm easily distracted by work tasks and a constant influx of email messages. Therefore, when I engage in social activities, it's always after work and outside my office, wherever that may be.

Once more, the Vision Map seems to naturally mitigate distractions through its inherent design. It wasn't a deliberate intention, but it's interesting how it effortlessly achieves that.

When tackling the daily tasks on your to-do list, you're motivated to efficiently complete them to achieve your financial goals, produce content, or deliver services. The Vision Map, designed to align with your vision, purpose, and objectives, inherently reduces distractions, allowing you to stay highly focused on your goals.

Generally, postpone viewing cute images or videos from friends or family until after dinner to avoid distractions. It's essential to request others message you later or wait, as I learned from an experience when a family member was at work and couldn't respond promptly. I felt humiliated and embarrassed and refrained from texting her again. Always remember that the person you're texting may have important work to focus on, so it's considerate to socialize and enjoy shared content after dinner.

When I am online, I usually remain focused on the task, often guided by my to-do list. This helps me stay away from distractions. Suppose a distraction takes more than a second, especially if it involves a video or unrelated content that doesn't contribute to my income. In that case, I quickly move on and return to my business tasks. I simply can't afford to look at cute images and videos because they disrupt my workflow and hinder my income-earning potential.

Once, I responded to the numerous messages flooding my Facebook inbox. One morning, after answering my emails, I devoted three hours to socializing and replying to everyone on Facebook. However, the outcome was disappointing. Nobody listened to my show, bought my book, left a kind review on Apple Podcasts, or became a genuine fan. Instead, 100 percent of the messages seemed to have ulterior motives, typically involving money or some other unsavory request. This experience taught me that devoting three hours to social media led to a big zero in tangible benefits. Since then, I've become more selective in what I choose to respond to.

Discussing this can be challenging because unless you're directly experiencing the ongoing changes, it's tough to enumerate them; sometimes, this can take years. Somewhere within your repertoire, you sell or develop products or services. That's pretty much the bottom line right there. I can't stress enough how often something has come along that changed the whole landscape, as you've likely witnessed during the madness of 2020 and 2021. I've encountered several instances impacting my business journey, and the sheer volume of changes to navigate is immeasurable. Without a clear vision, purpose, and well-documented primary objective, such as the Vision Map, you'll feel adrift in a stormy sea or be tossed around like a rag doll.

It's the only beacon when things take a turn for the worse, whether in business or your personal life. Having these key points firmly established doesn't make challenges easy, as disasters are still disasters. However, when you have a solid grasp of the eight key points outlined in the Vision Map, making the best decision becomes a no-brainer.

Usually, the right decision is the best one, although it's not always the case. Major life or business-altering choices can be unpleasant, but when something critical happens, the decision must prioritize the well-being of your life and business. Even when my business was hacked, and my domain was hijacked for pharmaceutical sales in Asia rather than reaching my podcasts, the decisions, though tough, were clear-cut.

Saying "build a house" takes just a few seconds, but the process can span months or years. The opposite is equally true, and that's the key point. If you struggle with staying on track or making decisions, it indicates you're not firmly grounded in your Vision Map steps. While they may take time to develop, once you have a clear direction in life or business, it's difficult to sway you.

Imagine planning a vacation. You've chosen a destination with your family or group, likely establishing your vision. The purpose is to enjoy the trip and gain experiences. Your objective might involve visiting tourist attractions. If a storm blocks your route or your vehicle encounters issues, it doesn't derail the vacation. You adapt by finding a detour or fixing the vehicle, as various challenges won't alter the vacation's core intent.

Consider a gas shortage scenario. You adapt by getting a gas can to ensure you have fuel. While you can anticipate some challenges, having a firm Vision Map lets you tackle whatever life throws your way. You risk ending up anywhere but your intended destination if you lack a clear vision, purpose, and objective. While such adventures might make entertaining YouTube videos, they won't necessarily align with your life and business goals for generating income. Unless you're independently wealthy and enjoy aimless driving trips for YouTube, the choice is yours to make.

Developing a disciplined mindset is simpler than you might imagine, and I'm confident about this. If your livelihood relies on creating and selling products or services, your mindset will naturally shift toward discipline. If you don't need the money, you have more flexibility, but the success of your business becomes uncertain. However, you might still create captivating YouTube content.

You might encounter employees or hires with that mindset—those who do the least while expecting the most. I've encountered such individuals in my business experience, and it's challenging. The solution ties back to earlier discussions, emphasizing the importance of patience. Even in dire financial situations, where you're uncertain about covering bills or buying groceries, patience remains crucial, as previously explained.

The key takeaway at this point is that you can initiate and grow a successful business regardless of your current situation, even if you lack financial resources. I bootstrapped my weekly show and elevated it to the level discussed earlier. This achievement was possible through the cultivation of a positive, disciplined mindset.

The two-column ledger is a critical tool for your business. It's a constant reminder of pending tasks that need your attention. This list remains within easy reach, urging you to take action. Heck, creating and sharing a graphic on three social media platforms to promote your latest show only takes fifteen minutes, leaving you with ample time for dinner! This simple accomplishment allows you to cross it off the list, eliminating future nagging. It's an enticing concept, providing motivation and enthusiasm even after a full day's work. How cool is that? Quite a paradox, isn't it?

Think of the ledger as your boss, directing you to complete essential tasks. Even if you're not happy about it, these tasks are the keys to your financial well-being, family support, and bill payments. They collectively dictate your life, making you your employee. You get to keep most of your income minus what goes to employees, subcontractors, taxes, and bills. That's a small price to pay for your happiness, isn't it?

It's essential to establish a well-defined vision, strong purpose, clear objective, and master plan divided into strategic and tactical steps. These constitute six of the eight steps necessary for a fully developed and highly successful Vision Map.

Our to-do lists hold us accountable, ensuring we take the initiative to accomplish tasks. While we might occasionally embark on adventures like aimless country drives for YouTube content, these activities usually don't generate enough income to sustain us. Therefore, we require more reliable income sources (unless we're on vacation).

Accountability is established by taking extremely small, baby steps toward achieving your goals. If you have an action to complete, break it down further. Everything can be categorized as a product or service with the intent to sell, rent, or lease. Essentially, anything you acquire is meant for future transactions.

Break it down into simple steps. Consider a course creation process. You need to outline your content, create and edit videos, ensure professional packaging, set up a sales platform, and establish branding with a logo and title; it's about a thousand steps. Develop a comprehensive master plan, including the strategic aspect, akin to a military mission to capture an island controlling a sea corridor. Your strategy involves taking control of that location. Then, meticulously plan the tactical steps required to execute the above tasks, much like the step-by-step approach to capturing the island.

Let's add a practical dimension to accountability. What can you create and sell in the next one to three months? This is the time for brainstorming. Starting from scratch and needing immediate income, consider crafting a mini-course in your area of expertise. With dedication, you could complete it in a weekend or two. This aligns with step 7 in the Vision Map. Accountability naturally falls into place as you work alongside your other business tasks, as this mini-course provides the income you need while building your business.

I'm not selling anything here; I'm emphasizing that accountability can become an integral part of your operations, functioning autonomously. It becomes your boss, guiding your actions. The point is to embed accountability in your workflow, let it be your taskmaster, and record these tasks on your two-column ledger. Assign tasks when necessary, but don't check them off until completed. Prioritize the most important tasks today, and for tomorrow, outline the next steps or write them down in your ledger. Each day, let your ledger guide you in assembling and selling your product or service, making it the driving force that keeps you on track.

Instilling discipline in a team can be difficult. I've experienced this firsthand, especially when managing large teams of over 100 people. It's an experience I'd rather not repeat, but it taught me valuable lessons. The nightmare was exponentially magnified when multiple bosses, often with conflicting ideas, were involved. However, they all concurred on one point: placing blame at the receiving end of the situation. (I wonder who that may be?)

In this catastrophe, bosses and their superiors lacked a clear vision, leading to constant interference and confusion—a real headache. If everyone had a well-defined vision, purpose, and objective for the company's direction, we wouldn't need to rely so much on Dr. Scholl's foot pads. I mention this because I've seen similar chaotic scenarios in my professional experience. Getting everyone on the same page is a crucial task that must be on your to-do list.

In my professional experience across various company sizes, one of the primary culprits disrupting discipline and causing chaos is the absence of clear and unified directions. By that, I mean multiple directions. Multiple conflicting orders often emerge, pulling the team in different directions, which can demoralize and overwhelm them. It's a real morale killer. It's essential to consider whether your company is simultaneously bombarding the team with multiple tasks. Don't take this lightly; it can be happening without your awareness. During a storm, your team might feel tossed around like a cork in the ocean. As I mentioned earlier, multiple simultaneous directives can significantly *damage* team morale. Let's emphasize and highlight this point.

Provide clear, simple directions and set priorities for your team; they'll appreciate it. The most effective way to achieve the best and quickest results is acknowledging when your team does something well. Neglecting to do so or showing a lack of acknowledgment can significantly impact morale. Consider spending time incognito with your team to understand their concerns. Make it a point to recognize their achievements when they happen. Be a tough boss when necessary, but don't forget to smile when it's deserved. I come from the old days of corporate America, and I can vouch for the power of acknowledgments. They boost happiness, productivity, and focus. Think about how your mood affects your work and the impact of a happy boss on your performance. Now, apply that level of contentment to your team.

Talking about resilience after making mistakes is challenging for me. Throughout my corporate career, I encountered numerous instances of receiving misguided directions from superiors that I had to follow. You might wonder why I continued working there, but there were many times when a decision seemed uncertain, not good or bad. I suspected it might not work. However, sometimes, I'd be surprised because it turned out to be exactly what the company needed. It's when decisions go awry that things get complicated and tough.

I've noticed that many of the issues I encountered in my career often resulted from following strong directions from upper management, which sometimes proved disastrous. I prefer not to point fingers or throw anyone under the bus. Sharing specific details is beyond my professional acumen, so I'll aim to provide a more general perspective.

I once managed the lead generation department for a company, and we were quite successful. However, the company's leadership made a side deal with another company to receive leads ahead of our clients and then sell the unused leads to our clients. It was indeed nefarious, and the company's top executives vehemently denied any such dealings were going on. Consequently, I found myself in the crossfire as clients complained that their leads were already used, and I had to truthfully deny any involvement.

Eventually, I decided to act as if I had been aware of this practice all along and suggested leveling the playing field to bring in more revenue. Some executives confided in me and supported the idea, which brought me great joy. Yet the next day, I faced a severe reprimand for my actions and for bypassing the top leader. In response, I quickly realized this team was not worth the further investment of my efforts. I soon resigned and left.

In situations involving missteps, you can only address what's within your control. After that, you need to engage in some soul-searching and question the worth of it all. What value does money hold when your integrity is on the line? What's the worth of money acquired through dishonest means? Staying would make me an accomplice, and I've always wondered, just as those who regularly engage in such complex situations: *What is the value of ill-gotten money?* I sleep extremely well every night. Staying might have brought more wealth, but it would have haunted me. When you realize you can no longer effectively pursue the right path, it's clear that it's time to move on.

As I explored different paths, I discovered podcasting. I combined my experiences to create a meaningful weekly show featuring elite entrepreneurs who generously shared their wisdom and guidance with the audience and me. Their weekly wisdom contributed to producing a successful show, landing it among the top 100 podcasts on Apple Podcasts. I'm grateful for the wisdom that allowed me to maintain my integrity and make the right choices. As I say on my show, "Sow good seeds and do good deeds," and join me on the next episode of *The Tony DUrso Show.*

ACTION STEPS

1. **Adopt a Simple and Consistent Task Management System:** The author highlighted the effectiveness of using a basic legal pad and pen for task management. This approach can be transformative for your business. Start by listing your crucial tasks in a simple format, like a two-column ledger, focusing on what aligns with your business goals and vision. This method offers simplicity and consistency, ensuring that you stay on track and never lose sight of what needs to be done.

Keeping a physical list with you at all times can serve as a constant reminder and can be more reliable than digital methods that may fail due to technical issues.

2. **Maintain Brand Consistency Across All Platforms:** The author emphasizes the importance of consistency in branding. This applies to your business as well. Ensure that all your branding elements, like logos, fonts, and colors, are consistent across various platforms. This uniformity helps in building a strong, recognizable brand identity. It's also crucial to communicate these standards clearly to your team, including any subcontractors or affiliates, to ensure that everyone is aligned with your brand's vision. Remember, consistency in branding shapes how customers perceive and interact with your business.

3. **Prioritize Patient and Clear Communication with Your Team:** The challenges the author faced in implementing changes and maintaining consistency underline the importance of patience and clear communication. In your business, practice patience and clear articulation of your expectations to your team. Understand that achieving unwavering consistency in your business operations may require repeatedly explaining and reinforcing your vision and objectives to your team. Remember, efficient communication and patience are key in aligning your team with your business goals and ensuring smooth operation.

ABOUT THE AUTHOR

A Top 100 Apple Podcast, the #1 show on Chartable worldwide (June 2022) and #1 on VoiceAmerica (over five years running), *The Tony DUrso Show* is routinely in the top ten internationally in various categories.

Launched in 2015 as *Revenue Chat Radio*, and eventually as *The Tony DUrso Show* on VoiceAmerica, Tony interviews elite entrepreneurs including Jack Canfield, Mark Victor Hansen, Kevin Harrington, and Wesley Snipes.

With over 40 million total listens, *The Tony DUrso Show* provides a massive impact for entrepreneurs who want to share with the world. In addition to weekly interviews, Tony's company provides social media marketing to help anyone gain more social media followers, and also grow their podcast. (Proper spelling is D'Urso but as search engines get confused, the ['] is dropped to make it simpler.)

FROM MILITARY INTERROGATOR TO BUSINESS INTERROGATOR

DANIEL HAMMOND

Is this what I want my life to be? I was twenty-three, holding the position of the most senior manager in my district at a major pizza chain, with over two years of experience, consistently working at least sixty hours a week.

As I pondered my future, I found myself in conversation with helpful Army recruiters. With top-tier military assessment scores, I inquired about the most challenging role available and ultimately enlisted as a Signals Intelligence Collector with Airborne and Spanish language guaranteed.

The Army honed my discipline. Basic training, in particular, was like a puzzle, where I had to balance following Army procedures, doing what was right, and finding efficient ways to bypass the standard protocols. For instance, during a weeklong training exercise, my battle buddy and I were assigned to a foxhole. It looked like it could rain, so to be better prepared, I strategically positioned our fallback spot between two trees, dug a trench to divert water, and built a protective wall to prevent water from flowing downhill.

After hours of digging, it became obvious that heavy rain was imminent. I took a brief two-minute break, snapping our two shelter halves together and discreetly tying it to one of the trees. If it hadn't rained, my initiative may have caused trouble. But as the rain began to fall in slow, heavy drops, I secured the other end to the second tree, protecting our dugout. We sought refuge in the hole together as the sky unleashed a torrential downpour. Approximately two hours later, our senior drill sergeant inspected our shelter and, almost smiling, said, "Carry on," indicating we were not in trouble. Throughout the night, the rain poured, leaving all the other soldiers drenched.

During those eight weeks, I embraced the Army way and reached the peak of my physical fitness. Then came Airborne school, a daunting challenge. The first day almost proved overwhelming. Each day in the initial two weeks started with a grueling four-mile run (six on Fridays). Despite being in the best shape of my life, that first test pushed me to my limits. Thankfully, I made it through, pretty drained. Unfortunately, the next test was thirty minutes of push-ups, sit-ups, and other fun Army exercises.

I hit a metaphorical wall hard. My vision dimmed, and I was desperate for water. After a brief rest and hydration, I pushed through to avoid being kicked out of the course. I couldn't fathom doing this for another nine days, but a cool staff sergeant advised me to drink a liter of Gatorade before sleeping and another upon waking. This made running and exercising more manageable and taught me the value of learning from others' experiences and being as prepared as possible for life's challenges. Eventually, I earned the title of paratrooper.

In Phase 3 of my training, I faced a six-month Spanish immersion course despite my struggle with learning languages. As I grappled with this challenge, an unexpected opportunity arose. Our unit's leadership needed a volunteer to represent us on the Soldier of the Month board. With no one else stepping forward, I hesitated momentarily and then decided to give it a shot, thinking, How bad can it be? During the board, I answered four out of twenty questions reasonably well. When the First Sergeant asked me at the end, "Hammond, did you study at all for these questions?" I said, "First Sergeant, I got here just two weeks ago, and my primary focus has been absorbing the basics of Spanish. I did not specifically study for this board." His follow-up question was, "Do you believe you could learn this stuff if given the opportunity?" I responded enthusiastically with a resounding "Yes First Sergeant!"

While awaiting the results, I asked about the performance of a fellow soldier. He said, "I think I may have missed one of the questions." I was very surprised to find myself as the winner of my company's Soldier of the Month board and I secured a third-place finish on the post that month, having answered nineteen out of twenty questions correctly. This taught me that such actions can lead to outcomes far beyond "just okay." Reflecting on my experience, I realized that stepping up when no one else would, doing your best, and being honest can yield exceptional results.

Consistency, to me, means more than just following routines. It's about my unwavering commitment to doing what's right, serving others to the best of my abilities, making tough choices, and prioritizing the common good when necessary.

If you ask those I've worked with, they might say I'm consistent in asking difficult or uncomfortable questions and injecting humor, even in crises. Ideally, they'd also say I tackle our most challenging issues head-on, take ownership, and consistently deliver exceptional results.

I've received a treasured compliment: "Everything you touch gets better." When I take on a role or a task, I focus on understanding its significance, who it serves, and its connections. I prioritize based on importance and impact, keeping an eye on potential escalation triggers. Recognizing when the seemingly unimportant becomes critical is important to delivering excellence.

Investing time to understand how your responsibilities affect other functions around you enhances your ability to serve effectively and become more valuable. Your value to those who rely on you is the key to expanding your responsibilities.

In my U.S. Army experience, I consistently sought to understand how my responsibilities connected with others. This led to me consistently serving in positions above my rank and taking on extra assignments during my fourteen years of service.

Excellence in a role requires connecting with those affected by it and understanding their priorities. For example, as a production manager, focusing solely on maximizing production can lead to issues like warehouse space shortages, quality decline leading to unhappy customers, and surplus defective products when important considerations are neglected.

My business partner, Dr. Ted Anders, has developed an organizational operating system called Customer Driven Leadership™ that ensures each function prioritizes what's essential for others. This aligned with my approach to serving effectively in my roles and was my motivation to co-author the legacy edition of *Customer Driven Leadership*.

When you take the time to truly understand people, their needs, and the organization's overall health, you're better equipped to find the least detrimental option in tough situations that benefit the whole. If you lack that consistent understanding, critical factors may be missed, and biases can misguide your decisions during a crisis. This is why I encourage leadership to proactively prepare for crises through simulations and "what if" questions.

I actively pursued the team's most significant challenges during my corporate America career. I have a passion for problem-solving, particularly relishing intricate and complex issues. For context, I typically handled tasks one-and-a-half to two times more complex than our standard workload—a significant challenge but still within the grasp of our capable team members.

In my final year, the project's complexity increased dramatically, initially by ten times and then by twenty times, due to a lack of requested resources. My role shifted from creating and presenting complex cyber scenarios to evolving a complex virtual technology platform. This involved scenario creation and realistic network construction, cyber security solution installation, customizations, exercise evaluation, tools design, and installation tied to specific objectives. Additionally, our red team (friendly hackers) had to build and test hacking attacks while managing various vendor solutions in the environment.

Finally, we had to develop scoring capabilities in a yearlong strategic process, progressing from rudimentary to basic, advanced, and eventually to incredibly dynamic scoring. None of these capabilities were present within my team, and I had just one assistant with their own workload of exercises to manage. While it may seem like an impossible task and a personal failure, the true lesson I learned is that the endurance challenge began not when I accepted the leadership of this initiative but when our executive leadership decided not to invest in its success despite its multi-year evolution.

Venturing into uncharted territory beyond your leadership's immediate attention can make you feel isolated. You bear the responsibility for success, and failure carries a price. However, if your leadership's superiors prioritize only checking off boxes, they'll likely allocate their time and resources to higher-priority initiatives.

Every successful step in my yearlong strategic plan pushed me further from our team's usual daily routine. I reduced the frequency of cyber exercises from four to one per quarter and introduced a higher level of complexity, presenting my leadership with more challenges than ever before. Success hinged on the specialized expertise of four or five other teams executing flawlessly in each project phase.

Even as I accomplished what was asked successfully, I often felt underappreciated. However, I understood that a single failure would jeopardize the entire year's progress, as it would compromise the foundation for the next challenge. So, I continued to work harder and harder and take the necessary steps to keep moving things forward.

As it turned out, I successfully completed the four exercises in building capabilities, but it felt like a lonely accomplishment. Even before reaching the finish line, it seemed that my leadership didn't truly appreciate the extent of my contributions to advancing our capabilities. I also sensed that, compared to previous years, they believed I complained too much and relied too heavily on their assistance in delivering the nearly impossible.

Despite a year filled with near-failures and weekly crises, my determination to fulfill my responsibilities and my unwavering commitment to the team, no matter the odds, kept me going. When I finally crossed the finish line, I realized that while I had achieved success by addressing the critical tasks, largely due to the amazing teams and talents I work with, I had grown well beyond my previous capabilities, rendering a return to my previous role impossible.

The year drained me, and I felt like nobody understood or cared about the project's long-term success. It was as if I had been assigned to create a luxury penthouse for a building that was scheduled for demolition. While my main motivation is to make a meaningful impact, this specific box remained unchecked. Fortunately, my other driving forces—serving effectively, learning, and personal growth—kept me committed until the end.

Ensuring I have time for the things that matter is a top priority. The definition of what matters varies from person to person and is shaped by individual values and passions.

A core part of my identity is being available to those who seek my help. I allocate calendar space to connect with the right people, using language that attracts like-minded people and repels those who don't align with my approach. My brand name, Business Interrogation, was a strategic choice. It's designed to appeal to those ready to heavily scrutinize their business operations. I add the most value when people are willing to honestly assess their business, and I can do so rapidly, but only if they commit to this process.

I received marketing advice, and some questioned the choice of the name Business Interrogation, as it may seem harsh. Many associate interrogation with what they see in movies, often involving coercion and torture. However, my real-world experience of interrogation is quite different. I approach it authentically, using honesty and finding common ground with those I interrogate. I do it honorably, taking care of everyone's interests to the best of my abilities, so it's not one-sided but a mutual exchange.

I value being available to the right people and dedicate time to being coached and surrounding myself with more knowledgeable people. I have gained great growth through the

10x Ambition Program™ from Strategic Coach®, led by Dan Sullivan. It focuses on entrepreneurial thinking and draws wisdom Dan's books with Dr. Benjamin Hardy like *Who Not How*, *The Gap and the Gain*, and *10x is Easier than 2x*, which focuses on eliminating 80 percent of your knowledge and actions to achieve ten times the level of growth. This program significantly influences my decision-making.

I also love Dan Sullivan's "always be the buyer" concept, which means not working with anyone who is not a good fit for you. My years at Strategic Coach have helped stretch my entrepreneurial mindset and ability to provide better service to my customers.

I'm also in a growth-focused mastermind group where we study self-improvement books and grow together as a community. We're a group of faith-based businessmen prioritizing gaining knowledge, supporting each other, and growing together. In addition, I play bass guitar in my church's contemporary service, which involves regular practice and commitment to serve at church. I'm also a member of a faith-based men's fellowship group where we delve into biblical and faith-based topics and share our personal struggles and family concerns.

I volunteer in an inner healing and prayer ministry where I lead or support a team spending four to six hours helping people understand their true identity and strengthen their connection to their Creator. This process involves letting go of false beliefs, forgiving past trauma, addressing generational issues, and seeking repentance for choices that hinder them from living the life God wants for them. Having experienced the profound liberation and inner peace this process brought me, I'm motivated to share this gift with others.

These are my most important weekly practices. I also period-ically engage in physical exercise, I was able to lose significant weight, but so far much of it has returned. I recognize the need for more consistent physical activity and healthier eating habits, and I sometimes make efforts in that direction. I firmly believe that prioritizing the good in your life leads to greater strength.

Dave Ramsay wisely states that if you're not controlling your money, it's controlling you. This principle also applies to focus and time. Time will slip through your fingers if you don't manage it.

I intentionally allocate time for what matters most to me, including coaching, personal growth, and connecting with global change-makers. I also ensure I have time for project work, recognizing the need to block it out on my calendar. Without this discipline, I'd probably procrastinate and work on it haphazardly. By scheduling it, I can complete it efficiently and have time for review and improvement, aligning with my commitment to serving my customers superbly.

When I'm intentional, and in that blocked time, I can mute notifications and silence my phone. Blocking time for family and friends is crucial to prevent work from intruding into personal life. During non-working hours, I avoid focusing on business problems. A system like Customer Driven Leadership ensures that essential matters are managed even when I'm not at work. Thoughtful and strategic delegation is key to maintaining focus in the digital age.

When it comes to consistency versus change, I strongly favor change. My core focus is innovation, and I'm driven to enhance businesses, as stagnation never leads to improvement. Even when a company is run well, I constantly seek ways to improve it while preserving what's effective.

When speaking with new clients, I prioritize their readiness in action, willingness to embrace disruption for stronger outcomes, and openness to scrutiny.

In my cyber exercises for companies, I walk executive leadership through realistic cyber disasters, prompting them to survive and thrive in challenging situations. These exercises help them anticipate and address potential issues before they arise, allowing them to identify and close security gaps. Just as fire drills in school prepare us for emergencies, practicing responses to cyber-attacks ensures a smoother and more efficient reaction when needed.

I believe people should consider what might threaten their success even in a thriving organization. This might involve hiring experts like me to simulate challenging cyber scenarios for crisis preparedness or engaging other professionals to explore different scenarios. Businesses that can weather adversity often come out stronger. Consider possible threats—for instance, a pandemic—and ask questions: Can employees work remotely? How would our operations change? What's the impact on our vendors and supply chain? How could we continue to serve our customers well? Do we have contingency plans if critical vendors fail? Can we pivot to alternative providers? What if a competitor disrupts our industry? How might they do it? How many customers might you lose? What's our response, and can we lead the disruption instead of trying to survive someone else's disruption? Explore game-changing ideas.

I love to come in when organizations are ready for a change. I'm here to challenge, clarify, and offer solutions, guiding the process. After we achieve successful results, clients can call me when they need my expertise again. The exception is entrepreneurs, who may need me on speed dial for their continuous innovation. Everybody needs change, and I excel in providing a unique perspective. I never knowingly accept a role to maintain the status quo; my forte lies in solving complicated problems without obvious solutions. Other people's problems are my playground. Stagnation is the first step toward losing market share. While some CEOs excel at maintaining the status quo, I believe that innovation is essential. It's crucial to recognize your strengths and avoid unsuitable roles. That's my perspective on the balance between consistency and change.

In terms of a disciplined mindset, I've focused on self-awareness recently. I find it fascinating to explore personality tests and self-assessments. These tools reveal insights into my behavior, strengths, service preferences, communication style, and more. I've taken numerous assessments, some of which have provided new perspectives on my self-understanding and how I'm wired.

To foster a disciplined mindset, first understand your identity, purpose, service style, who you want to work with, and your driving force, often referred to as your "why." Consider the relationships you want to be in, the challenges that inspire you, and what feeds your soul. After you understand that part, investing in coaching is valuable. Identify habits that get in the way of who you want to be. Acknowledge that everyone carries some level of brokenness. You can transform those experiences into strengths and superpowers by addressing and healing the brokenness.

Both Dan Sullivan and John Maxwell discuss the concept of "evaluated experience." This means not just dwelling on "what happened to me" but revisiting past experiences to extract lessons, taking responsibility if necessary (though not always), and using that wisdom to grow. It's about adding a new tool to your problem-solving toolbox, enabling you to navigate future challenges more effectively. For example, in the case of a recovered addict, realizing their previous lifestyle was unsustainable led to a profound transformation. Sharing this wisdom and understanding can be a powerful way to inspire and help others.

Unresolved issues, the struggles you "manage", and what you avoid can rob you of clarity and purpose. There are many paths to resolution. For me, it was inner-healing prayer and ministry work. Whether you label it as brokenness, limiting beliefs, enemy strongholds, addictions, or trauma, addressing these issues can lead to a stronger, clearer, and more whole life. You can achieve newfound clarity and wholeness by internally resolving them rather than perpetually grappling with them.

Knowing your strengths and weaknesses, sources of inspiration and distraction, and what you like and don't like to do provides the clarity and authenticity needed to become an integrated person. An integrated person doesn't juggle falsehoods of who they think they are; they accept themselves as they are, which enables them to serve people at a higher level with clarity and discipline.

Regarding accountability, my driving forces are a sense of responsibility to others and a commitment to serving people well and honoring my commitments. Failing people is unacceptable to me. Could an act of God prevent me from being successful? Yes, but I will do everything possible to be ready early and exceed expectations. I will try to do so in such a way that even if I don't have as much time as I think I will have, I will deliver results that exceed expectations.

I sometimes adopt systems to ensure success and integrate key lessons. An example from my life involves studying Army interrogation techniques, specifically their detailed question-asking methodology. This approach dissects even a simple statement like "I went to the movie" to extract every possible detail. By practicing this method for a certain amount of time, you can think about key lessons and apply them when needed. For example, it teaches you to ask detailed questions about something, such as who you went with, where you went, which cinema you chose, what movie you watched, and the precise timing. This method also helps gather in-depth information and discover connections within a statement, making it a powerful tool for acquiring insights.

Most people don't ask for that level of detail, but practicing that methodology has been useful in my everyday life. I've developed a knack for spotting missing or added information in casual statements and can explore what's relevant. By adopting this robotic questioning approach, I've become skillful at uncovering additional details in a conversation, allowing me to access important information more efficiently than others.

As another example, I was committed to losing weight but hit a plateau. I did the 75 Hard challenge, which required daily tasks: reading ten pages of personal growth material, two forty-five-minute workouts (one outside), a gallon of water, a strict diet, and a daily picture. Failing any of those things meant resetting the 75-day count! The program forced me to make better choices, and I ended up losing a total of seventy pounds. Even though I have regained much of that weight, I believe in my ability to lose it again and maintain a healthier lifestyle. Setting difficult goals and doing hard things will make you better.

When I look at team discipline, my usual starting points are team connection and setting clear expectations. For example, I was assigned a complicated signals intelligence tactical vehicle in the military and a team. One of our tasks was to disassemble and relocate the equipment within fourteen minutes. While some team members were recovering from injuries and limitations, we worked together around these limitations to find the best way to complete the task. Our goal wasn't to meet the standard but to outperform ourselves. Ultimately, we achieved a time of under eight minutes, nearly half of the standard time, and three minutes faster than similar teams in our unit.

During a training employment, one of my teammates and I watched a similar team using the same equipment, take over ninety minutes to break it down, unaware we were timing them. This experience reinforced the importance of team connection, ensuring clear expectations, and guiding them to comprehend the priorities that lead to success.

One of my business partners, Dr. Ted Anders, created the system, back in 1995, I currently rely on to inspire teams toward unparalleled efficiency and success. Known as Customer Driven Leadership, it serves as an operating system for high-performing organizations. It harnesses the talents of your team members and motivates them by gamifying your organization. People are rewarded for the success and evolution of the organization, as well as for exceeding customer expectations in ways that matter most to them. If you are not actively seeking input from your customers, it is difficult to truly understand what matters most to them.

Ask your customers, "What one thing would make you incredibly happy with our service to the point where you wouldn't want to work with anyone else?" Once you identify their top priority, ensure that every team and department in your organization improves at collaboratively delivering that solution. Implement a monthly check-in system that assesses how well each function met these "Customer Careabouts": Did you do the things you said you would do? Did you find ways to innovate and improve your customer delivery? Collaborative success generates incentive bonuses for the team, while teams falling short receive leadership support for improvement.

In entrepreneurial companies, these incentives are usually monetary.

I believe in hiring the right people with the right skills. However, rather than providing them with a strict list of ten tasks, I advocate helping them grasp their role in the organization's success. Encourage them to see the bigger picture, understand the functions of their team, and how they contribute to the company's growth. Share your vision for the company's future improvement. Also, take the time to understand their aspirations and incorporate their goals into their contributions to the company.

You'll likely discover various hidden gifts and talents within your company that can quickly enhance customer service. However, unless you ask, much like with your customers, you won't know someone on your sales team has a catering business on the weekends. Acknowledging this and asking them to cater your company's events can increase their fulfillment and lead to next-level success by channeling their passion. People love to work in areas where their talents shine. Whether you're gathering intelligence or building rapport with your employees, understanding their personal interests is crucial. By encouraging them to utilize their gifts and rewarding their contributions, they shift from being employees to becoming partners in the company's success. As long as you, as a leader, appreciate and honor them in ways that resonate, they will deliver new levels of success for you and your organization.

Innovation and adaptability define my core characteristics. I was flattered when a leader from another organization likened me to a Swiss Army Chainsaw, insinuating that I had the perfect tool or solution for all his specific challenges. We all also have our limitations, while a Swiss Army Chainsaw might be great if you want to build a log cabin, it might not be as effective for drilling a hundred-foot well or building a microchip.

My discipline wanes when I'm tasked with maintaining the status quo, when my gifts and talents are not being used, or when I witness an innovative solution being overruled by risk-averse decisions.

I accepted two senior positions that ended up not aligning well with either organization, albeit for opposite reasons. In one case, I saw the need for specific organizational evolution to ensure overall success at the next level. In the other, I offered risk analysis and strategic counsel on courses of action I believed were high-risk, potentially jeopardizing overall success. Despite my commitment to helping both organizations, it became obvious that my contributions did not align with their strategies. As a result, I chose to step down and redirect my efforts in other directions.

I believe that knowing your gifts, talents, and unique experiences helps you find positions that align well with you, enhancing your commitment and success in those roles. For example, my top five strengths in CliftonStrengths® are:

1. Strategic: The capacity to see multiple ways to accomplish a goal

2. Arranger: Proficiency in manipulating various variables to influence outcomes

3. Individualization: The skill to match specific roles with the right people

4. Connectedness: Making sure all important elements are integrated into devising the best solution

5. Maximizer: The ability to discern which solutions will provide the most favorable overall results

My talents shine when I focus on seeking, speaking, and solving problems. My flow state is when everything's on fire, and no one knows what to do. For example, I once led a technology-dependent event with senior executives from multiple Fortune 500 companies, and the technology did not work. When my wife asked how everything was going, I explained that I was having the time of my life despite the technology glitches and the pressure of managing a room full of senior executives with nothing happening the way it was supposed to go.

I did everything possible to mitigate the disappointment and maintain a positive outlook while managing expectations. Meanwhile, the technical experts worked nonstop to solve the issue. Day two went way more smoothly, but it felt less fulfilling for me since any good facilitator could have managed that day.

After the event, a senior executive told me that he knew I wasn't responsible for the technology failure. However, during the issue I kept saying that "we" were doing everything possible to resolve the problem, and he appreciated me taking ownership of a problem I did not cause. While it's flattering when someone important notices something you did well, the reality was that if I hadn't taken on the responsibility to face the problem, the stress on the technology team would have escalated dramatically. They probably wouldn't have solved the problem in time to salvage the event despite working the entire night to do so.

You can effectively navigate your weaknesses by dedicating yourself to excellence in your areas of strength. My discipline is demonstrated through three core components of who I am. First, my dad's advice, "If something is worth doing, it's worth doing right," has been a guiding principle in my life.

Its result is that I'm not the right person for the job if I can't do something right.

Second, I have a strong service-oriented nature. My ultimate goal is to serve well, and I find fulfillment in helping others be successful.

Finally, for those who may not possess natural discipline, I encourage them to rely on their strengths and values to overcome such challenges. My eighth highest CliftonStrength is Responsibility, which holds me accountable to others; my ninth is Self-Assurance, enabling me to persevere through tough times. My faith serves as a constant reminder that it is not solely about me and my success. These aspects help me overcome the reality that my second-to-last CliftonStrength, ranking thirty-three out of thirty-four, is Consistency, followed by my weakest strength of them all, Discipline.

ACTION STEPS

1. **Embrace Adaptability and Continuous Learning:** The author's experience in the military, particularly in transitioning from a military intelligence paratrooper to various challenging roles, highlights the importance of being adaptable and continuously learning. For yourself, learn and improve your strengths and create strategies to overcome your weaknesses. In your business, foster a culture where adaptability and ongoing learning are valued. Encourage your team to embrace new challenges and to view each obstacle as an opportunity to learn and grow. This approach can lead to innovative solutions and improved business practices.

2. **Implement Strategic Decision-Making:** The author's ability to strategically position and prepare for unexpected challenges, like the tactical decisions made during various types of training exercises, serves as a

powerful lesson for business leaders. Apply this mindset in your business by anticipating potential challenges and preparing strategic responses. This involves not only understanding the immediate implications of your decisions but also considering their long-term impact on the business. Regularly conducting scenario-based planning sessions can be an effective way to achieve this. When something goes wrong, identify the root cause and build an action plan around the lessons you learn from the experience, both positive and negative.

3. **Cultivate Leadership and Responsibility:** The author's journey from a pizza chain manager to leading teams in high-stress military environments underscores the importance of strong leadership and taking responsibility. In your business, strive to lead by example and encourage a sense of responsibility among your team members. This can involve delegating tasks effectively, providing opportunities for your team to take on leadership roles, and creating an environment where accountability and team success is valued and rewarded. By doing so, you'll build a more resilient and motivated workforce, capable of facing various business challenges head-on.

ABOUT THE AUTHOR

Daniel Hammond is the global leader in Business Interrogation. He drills into complex business problems, identifies what is hidden, and helps blueprint right-fit solutions that improve how businesses function and serve their customers like no one else in their industry. He is a paratrooper, expert interrogation instructor, and combat veteran with real world, global experience. He collaborates with global entrepreneurs and philanthropists to create solutions that make the world a better place.

Leading Through Adversity: Strategies for Organizational Success

Dr. Travis Hearne

Before I enlisted in the Marine Corps, my lifestyle was far from ideal. I was in poor physical condition, addicted to cigarettes, and frequently consumed alcohol to excess. My professional life was confined to the restaurant industry, and I was resigned to the notion that this was my unalterable destiny. However, the start of the Iraq war served as a pivotal moment, compelling me to reevaluate my life's trajectory.

The call to serve and defend my country was strong, but there was a glaring obstacle: my physical unpreparedness for military life. I was acutely aware that my current condition was incompatible with the demands of military service. Nevertheless, I made a solemn pact with myself. I committed that if I could endure the rigorous trials of boot camp, I would sever ties with my former self and the detrimental habits that had characterized my life up to that point.

Moreover, I vowed that as I ascended through the ranks in my Marine Corps career, I would strive for ongoing self-improvement as an individual and a leader. These self-imposed contracts served as my guiding principles, providing me with the resolve to navigate the grueling challenges of boot camp.

Ultimately, I succeeded in becoming a United States Marine, a milestone that stands as one of my life's most rewarding and transformative experiences. The physical and mental demands exceeded any challenges I had previously faced. Yet, my unwavering focus and determination fortified me, ensuring that no obstacle could deter me from achieving my goals.

* * *

In my organization, I emphasize four integral dimensions of health: physical, mental, emotional, and spiritual well-being. When diligently attended to, these principles culminate in what I term the "Holistically Healthy Leader." As someone in a leadership role, I consistently prioritize these four foundational pillars for several compelling reasons.

First and foremost, effective leadership is contingent upon personal well-being. My capacity to guide my team is compromised if I am not in optimal health across these four dimensions. Leadership is not just about directing others; it's about having the vitality and resilience to inspire and motivate. A leader who is drained physically or emotionally simply cannot lead effectively.

Secondly, my commitment to holistic health serves as a model for my team. It's akin to granting them tacit permission to invest in their own well-being. When I demonstrate a consistent commitment to maintaining a balanced life, it encourages my team members to emulate these practices. They feel empowered to prioritize their health, knowing it's valued within the organization.

The ripple effect of this focus on holistic health is profound. An organization that is consistently healthy across these dimensions is virtually unstoppable. I attribute a significant portion of our organizational success to our collective commitment to holistic well-being. This approach ensures that we show up punctually, fully prepared, and equipped to tackle any challenges that may arise. Our readiness is not just physical or mental; it's comprehensive, encompassing every aspect of our being. This holistic preparedness is the cornerstone of our organizational resilience and effectiveness.

* * *

When the COVID-19 pandemic forced a mass exodus from office spaces in 2020, our team faced a crisis of unprecedented proportions. Our leadership model had been meticulously crafted for in-person interactions, and suddenly, that entire framework was thrown into disarray. At that time, our team consisted of just eight members, and the uncertainty that loomed over us was palpable. Questions swirled in our minds: Would we ever return to our consulting roles? Had the era of conferences and keynote speeches come to an abrupt end? The future was a murky landscape rife with unknowns.

However, amidst the chaos, one thing was abundantly clear: we needed to adapt swiftly to the changing circumstances. Our survival hinged on our ability to pivot effectively. Our organizational culture had always been fortuitously rooted in crucial attributes like determination, trust, innovation, and an indomitable sense of grit. These core values were our guiding light as we navigated the challenges.

Seizing the opportunity presented by a nascent market, we began to innovate. We transitioned from our traditional in-person model to a digital platform, creating online leadership courses and webinars, often orchestrated right from our own backyards. Recognizing the strain other leaders were under, we also initiated a discounted coaching model to promote holistic well-being.

The credit for our successful transition goes unequivocally to our team. I took a step back and allowed them to leverage their strengths, trusting that they would excel in their respective roles. Their collective ingenuity and resilience enabled us to weather the storm and emerge stronger on the other side.

* * *

As I've often emphasized, transforming from mere motivation to disciplined habits has been a game-changer in my pursuit of holistic health. While motivation is a powerful initial catalyst, its impact is often transient. Elevating motivation into a regimented discipline is crucial to creating lasting change. When the objectives initially spark our motivation and become ingrained as daily disciplines, we unlock the potential to transcend our comfort zones and venture into unparalleled success.

Among the daily disciplines I've successfully integrated into my routine are mindfulness and dedicated time for meditation or prayer. These practices serve as an essential conduit for self-connection, allowing me to recalibrate and center myself. I engage in deep-breathing exercises to further hone my mindfulness skills and maintain a consistent relationship with a mindfulness coach.

Physical exercise is another cornerstone of my disciplined approach to holistic health. I commit to working out five times a week, varying my routine to include activities such as a six-mile run, a CrossFit session, or even a brief twenty-minute stretching regimen. This physical discipline enhances my bodily health and contributes to mental clarity and emotional stability.

One of the most invaluable additions to my holistic health regimen is counseling. I am an ardent advocate for this form of mental and emotional upkeep. Whether you label it "preventative maintenance" or "self-care," the impact is unmistakable: I am a more effective leader and fulfilled individual because of the insights and coping mechanisms I've gained through my counseling sessions.

* * *

In today's digital landscape, distractions are everywhere, always vying for our attention. Whether it's a breaking news alert every ten minutes or the allure of the latest Instagram reel, these interruptions can significantly impede productivity. Recognizing the detrimental impact of such distractions, I've implemented a series of digital guardrails to safeguard my focus and optimize my work efficiency.

One of the key strategies I've employed is using specialized blocking software on my work computer. This software restricts access to any non-work-related websites during designated working hours. While I permit myself the luxury of listening to music to enhance my work environment, I've successfully blocked access to potentially distracting websites, social media platforms—except LinkedIn for professional networking—and any streaming applications that could divert my attention.

The importance of implementing such digital boundaries cannot be overstated. Achieving sustained focus and productivity is an uphill battle without the aid of these technological tools. They serve as external enforcers of discipline, helping to maintain a conducive work environment.

Additionally, I've adopted a dual-phone strategy to delineate my work-life balance further. I maintain separate phones for work and personal use. Once my workday concludes, my work phone remains in the office, effectively signaling the end of my professional responsibilities for the day. However, I check my work phone at three-hour intervals and once before bedtime to address any urgent matters. This approach allows me to compartmentalize my work and personal life, reducing stress and enhancing overall productivity.

* * *

Change is the only constant in the ever-evolving landscape of the business world. Organizations are in a perpetual flux, and employee turnover rates are higher than ever. This underscores the importance of a strong organizational culture, encapsulated by the adage I wholeheartedly endorse: "Culture eats strategy for breakfast." This philosophy serves as the cornerstone of how I manage my business.

Our organizational culture is meticulously crafted to embody core values such as trust, innovation, creativity, kindness, strength, and adaptability. The objective is to create a resilient culture that can seamlessly adapt to external changes without compromising its foundational principles. Whether we're faced with economic downturns that necessitate budget cuts or periods of exponential growth—which we've experienced—our cultural ethos remains steadfast.

While it's true our culture undergoes periodic reassessments, particularly as new team members join and as the business environment evolves, the core values that define our organization remain unaltered. These values serve as our North Star, guiding us through the complexities and uncertainties inherent in the business world.

I think weathering the storms of change hinges on having a robust and adaptable organizational culture. A culture that fosters innovation and has the flexibility to adapt is indispensable for navigating the unpredictable waters of the business land-scape. This approach equips us with the resilience and agility needed to meet whatever challenges and opportunities come our way.

* * *

The significance of maintaining the right mindset in the journey toward success cannot be overstated. Without it, we risk aimless wandering and inevitable failure. One effective strategy I've employed to cultivate a focused and disciplined mindset involves setting goals at three levels: strategic, operational, and tactical.

Strategic goals serve as the long-term vision, spanning eight to ten years. These are the overarching objectives that guide the direction of my endeavors. On the other hand, operational goals are medium-term objectives with a timeline of four to eight years. These goals are crucial steps that bridge the gap between my tactical and strategic ambitions. Tactical goals are the immediate, short-term objectives that must be accomplished to pave the way for achieving operational and strategic goals.

The interconnectivity among these three tiers of goals is essential, but maintaining this synergy requires a mindset rooted in success and discipline. To ensure my goals are realistic and actionable, I adhere to the SMART criteria, making them Specific, Measurable, Achievable, Relevant, and Time-Bound.

However, even with well-defined goals, the journey can be fraught with distractions and obstacles. If my professional mindset deviates from my tactical objectives, the likelihood of achieving them within the stipulated timeframe diminishes, consequently pushing my strategic goals further out of reach.

To counteract this, I create detailed lists associated with each level of goals. For instance, if one of my tactical goals is to secure twenty-four speaking engagements and acquire three new consulting clients within a year, I go a step further by specifying the companies I aim to consult for and the locations where I'd like to deliver my speaking engagements. This level of granularity sharpens my focus and provides me with tangible action items, reinforcing a mindset geared toward success.

* * *

The concept of "life boards" has been a transformative addition to my personal and professional life. But what exactly are these life boards? Essentially, they are assemblies of trusted individuals who serve as accountability partners in various facets of my life. Each board focuses on a specific domain, providing checks and balances to ensure I'm on the right path.

For instance, my spiritual board is composed of pastors and esteemed members of my church community. Their role is to ensure that my actions and decisions align with my spiritual values, helping me maintain a close relationship with God. Similarly, my mental health board is vigilant in monitoring my psychological well-being. They are empowered to call me out if they notice any signs of deterioration in my mental health.

In the professional realm, I have a board that scrutinizes my career-related actions and decisions. They hold me accountable for meeting my professional goals and adhering to industry standards. Lastly, my life board consists of close friends who have a holistic view of my well-being. They step in when they notice inconsistencies or issues in any area of my life, be it personal or professional.

The rationale behind these life boards is straightforward yet powerful: external accountability is often more effective than self-imposed accountability. While it's possible to try to hold ourselves accountable for our mental health or business success, human nature makes us prone to rationalizing our failures. Inviting trusted individuals to serve on these boards diminishes the room for excuses significantly. These people have the courage to deliver hard truths and challenge me to elevate my performance and well-being. Their external perspective provides an invaluable layer of accountability, pushing me to be the best version of myself.

* * *

To cultivate a disciplined team, the first imperative is that I myself must exemplify discipline in both my words and actions. If I commit to doing or saying something, it's crucial I follow through on that commitment. Moreover, it's essential to communicate these expectations to my team. They need to know that they can rely on me to be consistent and disciplined, just as I need to know that I can expect the same level of commitment from them.

We've worked diligently to create a culture rooted in discipline and trust, which has been a cornerstone of our success. I trust my team to execute their tasks proficiently, and they, in turn, trust me to lead effectively and fulfill my own responsibilities. Establishing such a culture is not an overnight endeavor; it requires significant time and effort. However, once this culture is solidified, it becomes a resilient framework that is exceedingly difficult to dismantle.

It's imperative that these expectations are articulated from the outset and reinforced consistently. This doesn't entail punitive measures unless absolutely required. Instead, the aim is to foster an environment that naturally cultivates discipline and trust among team members.

In the competitive business landscape, often described as a "dog-eat-dog" world, it's not merely about survival but about thriving. To emerge as the best among competitors, our team must function as a disciplined, kind, and strong force of nature. This disciplined culture not only equips us to face the challenges that come our way but also positions us to seize opportunities, making us the "best pack of dogs" that gets the meal, so to speak.

* * *

One of the most profound failures of my life occurred during my time in the Marine Corps, specifically during our deployment in Afghanistan. I joined my first infantry unit in 2008, and almost immediately, a fellow Marine named Jake took me under his wing. Jake was a seasoned veteran, having been shot in a prior deployment to Iraq. We developed a close bond, relying on each other during the most challenging times. Our unit deployed to Iraq in 2008-09, and miraculously, we returned without losing a single Marine.

However, the real test came during our subsequent deployment to Afghanistan. Just two months in, tragedy struck: Jake was killed by an Improvised Explosive Device (IED). At the time, I was leading a team of Marines, and in the aftermath of Jake's death, my discipline morphed into uncontrolled rage. I drove my team relentlessly, obsessing over finding out how the IED was planted, who was responsible, and where they were hiding. After four days of this relentless pursuit, operating on minimal sleep and food, I looked up to see that my Marines were physically and emotionally shattered.

It was a gut-wrenching moment of realization. I had been so consumed by my own grief and anger that I had neglected to consider the well-being of my team, who were also grieving the loss of Jake and other injured comrades. My emotional breakdown followed; I found myself sobbing uncontrollably in my vehicle.

Knowing I had to make amends, I began with heartfelt apologies to my team. I acknowledged that I needed to grieve properly instead of channeling my emotions into destructive leadership. After giving ourselves the time to rest and recalibrate, we were able to re-enter the fight with renewed focus.

This experience served as a pivotal lesson in leadership for me. It fundamentally altered my approach to leading people, instilling in me a newfound respect for the emotional and physical limits of those I'm responsible for. I vowed never to repeat the mistakes I made during those dark days, and this commitment has profoundly influenced my leadership style ever since.

* * *

Life and leadership are complex journeys with challenges, setbacks, and crucial learning moments. Whether it's the discipline needed to guide a team, the balanced approach to personal well-being, or the lessons learned from failures, each experience contributes to our growth. Discipline stands out as a particularly vital trait, especially for a CEO.

Being a disciplined CEO offers numerous advantages that extend beyond the individual to impact the entire organization. It sets the stage for a culture where accountability, trust, and high performance are the norm. Such a CEO is better equipped to navigate the ever-changing business world, make informed decisions, and adapt strategies without losing sight of long-term goals. This disciplined approach filters down to every layer of the company, creating an environment where goals are consistently met, and challenges are tackled effectively. Additionally, a disciplined CEO can juggle the many responsibilities that come with the role, from managing stake-holders to strategic planning, all while maintaining personal well-being.

Adaptability is another key factor, given that change is the only constant in both business and life. By embracing discipline, clear goal setting, and a culture built on trust, one is better prepared to adapt to inevitable changes. Learning from past mistakes and applying these lessons strengthens your leadership approach, enabling you to navigate the complexities of both leadership and life with resilience, empathy, and effectiveness.

ACTION STEPS

1. **Embrace Holistic Health:** As the author demonstrates, integrating a holistic health approach into your leadership style can greatly benefit your business. Focus on enhancing not only your physical well-being but also your mental, emotional, and spiritual health. This comprehensive approach can improve decision-making, increase resilience, and inspire your team to prioritize their health, leading to a more productive and motivated workforce.

2. **Develop and Implement Life Boards:** Inspired by the author's strategy, consider forming life boards for different aspects of your personal and professional life. These boards, comprised of trusted advisors and experts, can provide valuable guidance and accountability. They can help you stay aligned with your goals, make better decisions, and ensure you are maintaining a balanced approach in all areas of your life, which can reflect positively in your business management and leadership.

3. **Cultivate a Culture of Discipline and Adaptability:** Apply the author's insights on the importance of

discipline and adaptability within your organization. This involves setting clear expectations, following through on commitments, and encouraging a culture where trust and discipline are valued. Such a culture not only helps in effectively navigating business challenges but also prepares your team to seize opportunities and adapt to changes, thereby enhancing overall organizational performance and resilience.

ABOUT THE AUTHOR

Dr. Travis Hearne is the founder and CEO of Titanium Leadership Coaching and Consulting (TLC), author of *Hybrid: A Guide for Successfully Leading On- Site and Remote Teams*, a Marine Corps combat veteran, co-founder of the Buffalo Leadership Academy, speaker, certified executive coach, corporate training creator and facilitator, organizational and cybersecurity consultant, father, husband, and son. Learn more about Dr. Hearne at drthearne.com.

STOP MAKING EXCUSES AND START MAKING COMMITMENTS

LUBA SAKHARUK

I had just been promoted to Director of Agile Transformation. I led a team of scrum masters and agile coaches, supporting over thirty engineering teams. I found myself responsible for ten careers, their salaries, their well-being, and the success of the teams they were supporting. If someone needed to be reassigned to a new team, it took many hours of conversation with various people on all levels of the organization to make it happen smoothly without hard feelings or escalation to upper management. While I was adjusting to this new role, barely keeping my head above water, I was approached by my boss and asked how I was keeping track of who was working on what and what progress was being made on each of the engineering teams we were supporting. I realized at that moment that I had no process in place to keep track of anything. This taught me to ask myself:

What type of questions will I need to answer a year from now?

What data do I need to collect now that will be useful in the future?

Collecting data throughout a project is important for several reasons:

- **Decision-making:** Data provides valuable insights that help in making informed decisions during the project's lifecycle. It allows project managers and stakeholders to assess progress, identify challenges, and adjust strategies accordingly.

- **Performance Evaluation:** By collecting data, you can measure the project's performance against predetermined objectives and key performance indicators (KPIs). This evaluation helps in understanding whether the project is on track and meeting its goals.

- **Identifying Issues and Risks:** Data can reveal potential issues and risks early on, enabling proactive measures to mitigate them. This prevents costly and time-consuming problems later in the project.

- **Continuous Improvement:** Data-driven insights facilitate continuous improvement by highlighting areas that require adjustments or optimization. This iterative process enhances project outcomes over time.

- **Accountability and Transparency:** Data collection promotes accountability by providing concrete evidence of project progress and outcomes. It also enhances transparency among team members and stakeholders.

- **Validation of Assumptions:** Data validates or challenges assumptions made at the project's outset. It ensures that decisions are based on actual observations rather than subjective beliefs.

- **Benchmarking:** Data collected from previous projects or industry benchmarks can be used to compare and set realistic expectations for the current project.

- **Evidence for Funding and Support:** Data-backed evidence increases credibility and justifies resource allocation when seeking funding or support for a project.

- **Learning and Knowledge Sharing:** Data collected during a project contributes to the organization's knowledge base. Lessons learned from one project can be applied to future initiatives, fostering continuous learning and improvement.

Data collection is fundamental to project management, enabling evidence-based decision-making, increased efficiency, and better project outcomes.

* * *

Let's explore consistency from a couple of angles: one from communication and working together and another from the benefit of recurring meetings and consistency in the meetings arena.

In my early twenties, I worked with a senior engineer who was very inconsistent in their behavior toward me. I was praised one day and made feel like I knew nothing the next. I held off confronting this individual until I could no longer take it. As I considered the best way to give them feedback, I realized that the inconsistency bothered me the most. When I gave feedback, it was apparent that if they believed I was not qualified for the job, I would have loved to be mentored and asked to stop praising me as it sent mixed messages that I didn't know what to do with. We became friends, and I learned the importance of being consistent when communicating with others. I adopted the practice of establishing working agreements, where each team member, including myself, shares what we love the most about working together and what upsets us. It is an open conversation that leads to a consistent set of rules of engagement with no surprises along the way.

Regarding consistency in the context of recurring meetings, I was recently nominated to receive a grant to support a mentorship program I have for Women In Tech. The woman pitching the RALM3 Mentorship Program asked many questions; one in particular stood out to me. She asked when the program was established, how many women participated, and how often we met. She was impressed when I said we had been meeting once a week since January 2023 and would continue to do so until the end of the year before reassessing and choosing what to focus on in 2024. Our community is growing, and at this point, because of the consistency of our meeting time, people know to schedule other things around when they want to join.

The same applies when putting processes in place in the work environment. I continue to consult with tech companies on agile methodology and scrum framework and train folks on various recurring scrum ceremonies (meetings) that are always at the same time and on the same day with specific agendas and desired outcomes.

Consistency matters when scheduling recurring meetings for several reasons:

- **Time Management:** Consistent scheduling helps participants plan their time effectively. When meetings occur at predictable intervals, attendees can allocate time in their calendars in advance, reducing conflicts and ensuring attendance.

- **Establishing Routine:** Regularly scheduled meetings create a sense of routine and structure. This fosters a more organized and efficient workflow, as team members know when to expect updates, discussions, and collaboration opportunities.

- **Reduced Confusion:** Consistency in scheduling eliminates confusion and prevents misunderstandings about meeting dates and times. Participants can rely on the established schedule, reducing the likelihood of missed meetings or last-minute rescheduling.

- **Increased Accountability:** When meetings occur consistently, attendees are more likely to take them seriously and be accountable for their participation. This can lead to better engagement and more productive discussions during each meeting.

- **Maintaining Momentum:** Recurring meetings help sustain the momentum of ongoing projects or initiatives. Regular check-ins allow teams to monitor progress, address challenges, and keep projects moving forward without unnecessary delays.

- **Long-term Planning:** Consistent scheduling aids in long-term planning. It allows teams to align their work and deadlines with the meeting cadence, ensuring that essential milestones or deliverables coincide with the appropriate discussions.

- **Respect for Participants' Time:** Establishing a predictable meeting schedule shows respect for participants' time. It minimizes the need for last-minute adjustments or rescheduling, which can be disruptive and frustrating.

- **Cultivating Team Collaboration:** Regular interactions through consistent meetings foster a sense of collaboration and teamwork among participants. It enables better communication and strengthens team bonds over time.

- **Adherence to Agendas:** Consistent meetings make participants more likely to adhere to meeting agendas. They know when to prepare and what to expect, leading to more focused and productive discussions.

Consistency in scheduling recurring meetings brings various benefits, including improved time management, increased accountability, reduced confusion, and enhanced team collaboration. It contributes to a smoother workflow and better overall project management.

* * *

My most recent challenge was when I didn't have a single person sign up after six months of hard work putting together a retreat. I invested thousands of dollars in my assistant's salary alone, who was putting together all the marketing materials, building a website page for it, and many other tasks. Organizing an event is a pure pleasure for those who love it, but it is a lot of work. The original vision was to offer a retreat for Women in Technology who want to grow in their careers. It was supposed to have three tracks:

1. For those who are already in tech and want to get to the next level

2. Those who have perhaps retired from the military and were looking to get into the tech space

3. Those ready to get out of the tech space and launch their businesses.

All the trainers were lined up, and no one signed up. Every discovery call I had led to yet another expert looking to share their craft and be a trainer. The ratio of trainers to attendees was 7:0.

One morning, it came to me. There was a clear vision (although the original vision was also clear, so I wasn't falling into that trap again of being absolutely sure it would work). I asked in various channels if there would be interest to have a mastermind. Plan C was also to open it up to all, not just women.

Plan B meant that rather than be focused on women in technology, make it about each trainer who would attend. Find out what outcome each trainer would want from the retreat/mastermind and match them with other trainers with the proper skill set to help. Within two weeks, it was 75% full, with three more months before the retreat and various forums where I planned to share about the retreat in front of hundreds of women.

* * *

I like to start each morning with "me" time. I either go for a long walk or pour myself a cup of delicious coffee and if weather permits, drink it outside. I check my calendars the night before and know a rough plan for the next day. I still juggle being a full-time senior lead consultant, so I prioritize my full-time job from 9:00 a.m. to 5:00 p.m. Most of my networking or discovery calls are scheduled before 9:00 a.m. or after 5:00 p.m. All my writing projects, such as keynote speeches or books, happen on the weekend. The RALM3 Mentorship Program occurs on Tuesdays. I have a recurring call from 4:30 a.m. to 5:30 a.m. and allocate the rest of the evening for any 1:1 sessions related to the program. Of course, if there is a family emergency, that is prioritized over all else, and there is always a plan B in place. The most important habit is to listen to my body and mind and ensure batteries are recharged before they run out. Health is the number one priority.

* * *

If you could see the screen time daily usage on my cell phone, the data would immediately disqualify and discredit me from answering the question of how to manage and maintain digital discipline. I am on my phone more than I feel I should be, and in all honesty, focusing is often difficult. With that said, I have set clear priorities when it comes to phone usage and getting projects done.

When I run a training session, my focus is on the attendees. If I am in a 1:1 mentorship session, I focus entirely on the other person.

If I am in person at a meeting with hundreds of attendees and what is being discussed is irrelevant to me, I allow myself to get distracted and check emails and answer texts. But I am also aware that I might be sending a message to others that I don't care if I am not engaged. It's a slippery slope. This is a balancing act. Even if what is being discussed is irrelevant to me, I will not be on my phone the whole time. I will allow a few minutes here and there, but that is it.

The most important time to focus and not get distracted is with writing projects, so I allocate uninterrupted time for those.

When I have to write keynotes or work on a book, I will allocate time to write an outline first. With that, I will start thinking about it while I walk, hike, or swim; it doesn't have to be all sitting in front of the laptop. I will come up with an idea and send myself an email with a few sentences. When enough of those small chunks are thought through and gathered, I will allocate an hour to sit down, put away all other devices, and glue all the pieces together. Given that I have been able to publish a couple of books, contribute to four, and deliver a few keynotes, I know this process works.

* * *

I had mentioned earlier how effective it was to hold Zoom calls constantly for over six months as part of the RALM3 Mentorship program. The weekly Zoom calls started in January of 2023 when I created a course on teachable called "How To Be Change Architect." I felt a self-paced course was necessary, and supplementing it with live calls would benefit people with different learning styles. I also wanted to have meaningful conversations on various topics and have them recorded in case we could use some of the nuggets in the future. Calls were never mandatory, and we never knew how many people would show up. It was going so well that when we finished a third eight-week cohort, I decided to extend the Zoom calls until the end of the year.

Come August, I noticed the attendance was low, but yet still useful for many. My rule was that if at least one person showed up and got value out of it, then it was worth my time. By August, I also got accepted to be a TEDx speaker, had a few business trips planned, and the sign-ups for a retreat I organized were going full swing. I made a tough call that went against my previous promise. I put the Tuesday calls on hold until September. I broke the consistency, which was not easy, but I had to admit that I needed to reprioritize. Priorities change. Market changes. Change is inevitable, and so is pivoting.

* * *

While working with my publishing and business coach on my memoir, I experimented with various suggestions for being more disciplined. It was my first big writing project, and I admit I did not know what I was doing. By nature, I am more of a "go with the flow and wing it" type of person. With years of experience and leadership roles in the corporate world, I became more disciplined, but it is all in comparison. I have worked with people who were so disciplined and organized that, in comparison, I looked like I was winging everything. Then, I met a few people compared to whom I was the most organized and disciplined person. This is what I learned along the way:

There is no right or wrong way.

Your way is the right way.

Do what works for you.

Do you see results? Have you finished projects? Are you able to achieve outcomes? If yes, even if your mind is all over the place and seems to jump around and not be disciplined enough to your satisfaction, know it doesn't matter. If it works, then it is all good!

If you want improvement in finishing projects, I highly recommend working with someone who can hold you accountable. Look for mentors. Ask for help. Often, knowing that someone will ask you tomorrow about the progress you made today will help you carve the time out, focus, and finish the task at hand.

* * *

In my book, *How to Fyail in Digital Transformation*, eight contributing authors and I, all women in tech, dedicated a whole chapter to mastering accountability.

I share that nothing drives me more bananas than someone not delivering on their commitment. Blaming others would have to be second in line, but this chapter in the book focuses first and foremost on accountability. We talk about personal accountability, accountability for the culture of the organization, as well as accountability for a digital transformation. Here is an excerpt from this chapter where Vita is the character in the book based on me in real life,

"This is extremely frustrating," Vita shared. "I understand that people have different levels of passion for the work they do, and it is not about Type A personalities, I am talking about accountability. It is not just about taking pride in the work you do but having respect for the people you work with. What makes someone just ignore a deadline and not even mention that they don't plan on delivering what they committed to? More than that, when asked, they blame it on other teams. It is always someone else's fault. There is a pattern now that I am observing."

"Listen," said Olivia with a very calm voice. She could tell Vita was boiling inside. "Lack of accountability does often become a blame game, but I think we often fail to recognize that the word itself, the meaning of accountability, could be interpreted and internalized differently for different people. So, individual behavior comes from each person's own definition of accountability."

"That's an interesting thought," Vita said, now a lot calmer than before. "It seems so straightforward to me. If you say you will do something, you get it done. I guess this is my definition of accountability. I like things simple."

If anyone is looking to dive deeper into this topic, I have created a course based on this book and all the concepts, which allows for self-paced content consumption, real-time discussion of each topic, and Zoom calls with myself and other book co-authors. It can be found at https://ralm3.teachable.com/p/digital-transformation-lesson-learned.

For me, it is about commitment. If I made a promise, unless I am in a coma, there is no excuse for not delivering on the commitment or not communicating that I won't be able to deliver on the commitment. Of course, we all drop balls occasionally when we over-commit. Once in a while, it is okay. There is a way to recover from that without damaging your reputation.

However, it is a major problem when not being accountable to yourself and others becomes a pattern and consistent behavior.

I have a rule when it comes to people not being accountable when working with me. I give the benefit of the doubt. I offer help multiple times. If I see that someone isn't being accountable and isn't accepting the offer to help to be more accountable, I simply do not do business with them.

* * *

I learned over a decade of being in various leadership roles that accountability and discipline come from within. It cannot be forced. I believe in leading by example, so I lead by delivering on my commitments or promises. I also believe that having a clear vision of where you are going and communicating it clearly helps with discipline and accountability. Knowing what brings joy to each team member and what will make them want to come to work every day or want to work on a specific project is also a huge factor in how disciplined and consistent they are.

* * *

I see everything as a learning opportunity. If you have that mindset, no matter what happens, you know you have gained experience and are now stronger and more resilient to tackle the next challenge.

I had a vision in August of 2022 to publish a book by August 2023 on how to be a change architect. Based on my previous experience collaborating with others on a book, I decided to take a new approach. I envisioned having each contributing author write a few blogs, which I would then glue together and make a book out of. I had thirteen people lined up, and they were all very excited. Plus, it was at no cost to them. It was my way to take folks on a journey of boosting their credibility as authors and experts in their fields. It was very organized. I had a Slack channel going. I offered 1:1 brainstorming and writing sessions.

About five months later, after many attempts to ignite the initial enthusiasm and only a handful of blogs written, I had to drop the idea and pivot. I failed to bring my original vision to life and keep people passionate about the project. I had to remind myself that FAIL means Facing Another Important Lesson. I decided to take another approach and create a course called *How To Be a Change Architect*. The thought process and new vision was that I would take folks on a journey of this course, create an outline, have one-hour Zoom sessions, and then that can be transcribed and made into a book. Out of the original thirteen, only ten went through that course.

By August 2023, we still do not have that book published. Yet. However, the journey was full of lessons, great discussions, and relationship-building. As leaders, we need to know when to pivot. No matter how grand our visions may be, if something is not working, we need to know when to decide to pivot and develop a new vision. We need to put our egos aside and know that deciding to pivot when you have your mind and heart set on something is part of being an effective leader and a change agent.

ACTION STEPS

1. **Implement a Robust Data Collection and Management System**: Your business can benefit significantly from adopting a systematic approach to data collection and management. This action involves setting up processes to gather, analyze, and use data to inform decision-making. By doing so, you'll be able to evaluate your project's performance, identify and mitigate risks early, and ensure continuous improvement. This system will also enhance transparency and accountability within your team, thereby boosting overall productivity.

2. **Establish Consistency in Communication and Meetings**: Consistency is key in business operations. You should aim to develop clear and consistent communication channels and working agreements within your team. This can involve setting specific rules of engagement to avoid misunderstandings and ensure everyone is on the same page. Additionally, adopting a routine for recurring meetings – with fixed times and agendas – can improve time management and team collaboration. This consistency helps in maintaining momentum and ensures that your team is aligned with the project's goals and timelines.

3. **Embrace Flexibility and Adaptability**: While consistency is important, your ability to adapt to changing circumstances is equally crucial for business success. Be prepared to reassess and pivot your strategies when necessary. For example, if a particular project or initiative isn't yielding the desired results, don't hesitate to explore alternative approaches or adjust your goals. This flexibility not only demonstrates strong leadership but also helps in optimizing resources and maximizing opportunities in a dynamic business environment.

About the Author

Luba Sakharuk, a Worcester Polytech Institute of Technology graduate with a master's in Computer Science, transitioned from software engineering to agile coaching, facilitation, and leadership roles in digital transformations. As a Sr. Lead Consultant, she authored two books and established RALM3 Consulting LLC, offering services in public speaking, facilitation, and mentorship. Residing in Framingham, Massachusetts with her family, Luba enjoys skiing at Loon Mountain, New Hampshire, and strolling along Craigville Beach on Cape Cod in her leisure time.

The Role of Resilience in Overcoming Business Obstacles

Chad Bruckner

I served in the government for twenty-one years—thirteen in the police force and eight in the military. I was a combat infantryman in the military and an undercover officer for the police force. Developing grit and resilience was something that just came with the territory. Additionally, I grew up on a low income and had to fight, and those lessons and experiences helped build resilience.

A test of discipline I experienced was in 2019 when I went through a work event, and I was reassigned and sent to a different patrol platoon, which I wasn't expecting. It was an organizational betrayal that I experienced, which put me in a position where I had to make a tough choice. Do I stay in this organization, or do I leave? Do I stay in this profession, or do I switch careers?

I fell back on two of my core values, which are non-negotiable to me. One is discipline. In this case, discipline meant charting a path forward and relying on my belief in myself, those around me who are in my corner, and the skills, training, and experiences I've developed. This discipline led me to make a hard choice to leave my agency, to leave the policing career outright, and to become an entrepreneur. I chose to chart a path forward into business and test myself to see what I'm capable of.

Some of the habits that I relied on were my values—the non-negotiables. I charted a path with my why and my destination in mind, which is so critical. We can't push through hard experiences unless we have a why and a vision of how we will do that.

Additionally, charting a path forward required me to focus on the relationships with people in my life who are in my corner, people who are change agents, people who are encouragers, and people who push forward. It was important to set healthy boundaries and cut out people in my life who were not on my side or did not have my best interest in mind. However, I had to make sure I kept people in my life who were honest with me and could hold me accountable and tell me the hard truths that needed to be said. Those things are very, very important.

Consistency is crucial when influencing other people in the organization trying to provide services and products that add value to clients and customers. It's imperative to be consistent. The benchmarks I've tried to incorporate into my life and career have been things like being highly self-aware and understanding that self-awareness is crucial to understanding ourselves. When we're up, how can we maintain? What can we do to bring ourselves back up when we're down? Self-awareness is crucial because to be consistent means understanding we are humans and have periods or seasons when we're not performing at our best. It also means understanding those seasons won't last forever. What we do today matters, so we must continue showing up daily. That's paramount. Regarding the larger perspective of embracing the journey, we must understand that the outcomes may not always be what we want. Still, if we're on this road for the long haul, we understand consistency is vital to getting where we want to go.

Two important things help maintain consistency. The first is having a why and understanding your mission. Focusing on your why and mission will help keep you on track like the guards on a bowling alley lane. They help us stay within our lane and stay balanced and focused. The second is passion and finding where your passion lies. Figure out how your passions can intersect with the corporation and find ways to align your momentum and contributions with your organization. Knowing your why and your mission and being passionate about what you're working toward keeps us moving in the right direction. And when we have our down seasons or moments of failure, our mission and passion will help us get back on the horse and keep moving.

Being resilient in the face of challenges is everything. As a business owner and CEO, challenges and obstacles are a part of life and business. Therefore, it is important to understand the challenges that will inevitably come and have systems in our operations and lives to deal with them. We do not need to fear the unknown or the obstacles that will come. That's where resilience comes in; it is about embracing all those failures and obstacles and wanting them to come.

Nobody wants the pain and discomfort that these obstacles bring, but we can know and understand that on the other side of that pain and discomfort is a lot of post-traumatic growth. There are lessons to be learned and the potential for stronger relationships, partnerships, better earnings, and increased organizational health. It is important to embrace challenges and rise to push through these obstacles, not stop at them, but find ways to chart around them, through them, and over them. Having a cash flow issue in my first couple of years of business was crucial to helping me learn these hard lessons.

Being new to entrepreneurship after twenty-one years in government and not having strong mentors to help me, although I had some people help me along the way, these are lessons I had to figure out on my own. One of the biggest ones was cash flow and lack of access to cash. I had to bootstrap. I also had to learn how to create an established business with operations. At first, I didn't understand what that looked like and how important it was to keep momentum in operations. The last thing you want as a CEO is to have operations halted or slowed down because you can't meet the bottom line or fill orders. Those are cataclysmic; they cannot happen. Those are issues I had to learn to push through in the beginning—how to bootstrap successful ongoing projects, use retainers, and focus on every cent we're spending to ensure we can be viable and sustainable.

To be a successful entrepreneur and business owner, you must have a strong base of discipline. To be disciplined, you have to know who you are. You have to know your strengths and weaknesses. Knowing yourself and having a robust process in your life to keep you on track and disciplined is how to generate momentum.

I experienced a lot of hard situations and environments while working in the government for twenty-one years. I've learned to incorporate several tools into my daily life, such as prayer, meditation, and reflection. As human beings, we make mistakes every day. And as CEOs and business owners, we want to pretend we're not human. We want to pretend those mistakes don't happen. I've learned to embrace those mistakes. I've learned to say "I'm sorry" daily. I learn from those lessons, reflecting on my mistakes and considering how to improve them next time. This is a trait I've noticed in the disciplined people I've encountered.

The most disciplined people embrace imperfection. They embrace the journey. They embrace the fact that they want to get better. They use that disciplined mindset every day to seek feedback, study the behaviors of others, and solicit feedback about how they can be better. This is what disciplined people do; they understand that what I do today matters tomorrow. What I do today affects future goals, and it's understanding that not having a down season today indicates future earnings. Doing this requires daily processes and routines to help us maintain discipline. We incorporate routines like prayer, meditation, reflection, and spending a lot of time on personal growth and reading and watching content that can enrich us. Our job as a CEO and visionary is to get things done and keep the ball moving, but we can't do that if we're not healthy and well. And how we do that—how we become well—is putting things in our daily process that humble us and help us grow.

Staying focused and conquering digital distractions in this modern world is one of the biggest challenges I've encountered for myself and in interacting and dealing with other CEOs and executives. Having a strong foundation of where you want to go and being goal-oriented keeps you on track and focused through those periods when you get heavily distracted, whether it's a news cycle or a time when you want to share some amazing projects you're working on as a company.

Digital distractions are around us every day. Incorporating a set morning or evening time to address social media and leveraging people in our companies to help can help us stay on track. As the CEO, we cannot be bogged down in the social media world. The solopreneur journey that is becoming so prevalent in content creation and social media marketing is very powerful because 80 percent of their work is online and on social media; therefore, their marketing must connect with their prospects and be focused on building their following online. So, of course, you will have to spend a lot of time online. However, if you're not in a role where you're driving social media numbers and your business is an online business, you have to spend your time on what your tasks of the day are in leadership and influencing the team, making sure everybody's moving in the same direction. It's, therefore, important to cut out distractions if you want to affect the bottom line.

Operating in constantly changing environments and meeting the demands of your clients and customers are among the most profound skills you can have as a CEO or business owner. As visionaries, we must plan for what we want to do. We must forecast what we think we need to do. Yet, change is inevitable. They say the best-laid plan is great until it begins, and everything falls apart. These things are true. This happens all the time, and changes are inevitable in business.

Knowing your values and who you are helps you weather those storms and not be on such a pendulum swing or yo-yo ride. Developing confidence as an individual and CEO helps us push through changes. Even good change can be challenging if you're not prepared for it. The best CEOs can sit amid these changes and inconsistencies—both good and bad. They know how to meet the demands of both environments and are flexible. Sometimes, we must be rigid. We have to stand for what we believe in. But other times, we have to be limber. We have to pivot and roll with the environment. The best leaders and CEOs can do that.

It's also important to understand that change is normal. Frustration, annoyance, and other emotional reactions to change only hold us back and prolong the change or environment. Sometimes, we must make a move if we want to improve things. Sometimes, we must be the change agents ourselves. It can be scary when we recognize that change needs to happen, and no one around us is doing it. Our job as visionaries, leaders, and executives is to make hard changes. We all love consistency. We value and preach consistency. We teach it. We encourage everyone to be consistent. Yet, change is inevitable and happens daily in our companies, so we must be able to meet the demands and challenges of change. That's a hard thing to do, to want to be consistent but also embrace the opportunities for change. If you can live in the middle of that, you'll be on the good road to success.

The most important thing we can do as leaders in business, military, law enforcement, or whatever we're pursuing is maintain a growth mindset that is focused and disciplined. Our mindset is the force that will drive everything. Everything flows through our emotional responses, mindset, and ability to receive information quickly, formulate a plan, and execute it with the resources and people we have. That is the crux of moving and operating at a highly efficient and successful level.

How do we do that? You have to feed the mind. You have to feed it with positivity. You have to feed it with encouragement. I have learned to chase the margins. One-inch margins are on each side when you print on a piece of paper. If we print with one-inch margins every single day for our lives, there is all that wasted white space on one inch all around the borders of our pages. But what if we set our printer parameters so the words go left, right, top, and bottom to the edge. Think of how many more words could fit on each page. Think of how many more experiences could fit on each page. Think of how many more lessons we can add to that one sheet of paper. If we do that every day and develop a consistent approach, think of how much more we could add. That's how I approach mindset. I try to feed it with as much knowledge and intuition as possible, but I also understand that practicality is important.

Too many of us read too often and do less. I've worked to embrace the academic part of growing the mind while balancing action, being in the field and the real world, and applying everything I've learned, read, and experienced. I've learned that success lied to me through all those trials and tribulations. It was the failure that I learned the most from and the failure where my mindset benefited the most and grew the most through those hard lessons.

Additionally, great people who chase excellence desire the truth and accountability of good people. They want to be around people who are always truthful with them and hold them accountable. And that's what I've tried to do to embrace and develop a disciplined mindset.

Personal accountability is one of the most important things in running a successful organization. From police chiefs to military commanders to entrepreneurs and CEOs, if we can't hold ourselves accountable to the standards we set for our company, how can we expect others to meet those demands and standards? Conversely, if we are trying to hold people accountable for what we don't do ourselves, that inauthenticity and lack of being genuine will create a lot of turnovers in our companies. We'll make retention and filling key spots in our companies something that requires our constant attention and disrupts our momentum.

Enforcing accountability starts with yourself. It starts with holding yourself to the highest standard possible. And for me, I've always done that. There is not a soul in the world who can hold me to a standard higher than myself. My value structure has reigned supreme. I have dog tags around my neck that I wore in the military that remind me about the importance of respect, loyalty, honor, discipline, and duty. These are things that drive me, and this is what helps me hold myself accountable. When I make a mistake, you don't have to point it out to me; I'll come and tell you that I made a mistake. Leading by example and influencing people in our teams is a big deal. We influence our teams because they see that we're the first ones to admit our mistakes; we lead by example, and that creates positivity. If we could do that daily, it would create a positive environment in our workplaces.

The last thing I incorporate is a code of conduct. This is a personal code of conduct, and I incorporate this into every aspect of professional and personal dealings. I have a ten-point bullet list I incorporate into everything I do. One of them is I will always be truthful with my teammates. I will always give more than I take. And there's ten of these on this code of conduct, and I hold myself to these standards. I live by that. I lead by example. And I hold myself accountable to these standards. I've been a part of some highly successful and performing teams because we all embrace this mindset, accountability, and discipline. Being personally accountable to yourself and your teammates is a fundamental and paramount criterion for healthy, successful, and sustainable organizations.

Leadership is more than influencing the team toward a common objective and goal. Every organization needs managers and supervisors. These are taskmasters who are trying to move the day-to-day operations. However, we also need leaders. We need visionaries. We need people who influence others through their example and actions. This is how we build momentum and create high-level services and products that drive innovation and disrupt marketplaces.

Leading by example is a core capability and fundamental in leadership. You have to lead by example. When we lead by example, do what we ask, and expect our teammates to do, we remove any obstacles or barriers to accomplish those tasks. We put it back on each teammate based on their capabilities if they've been trained or developed properly to achieve those tasks. We remove any excuses that will create toxic environments that prevent people from achieving and performing well. Leading by example is huge.

In my experience as a military combat leader and undercover detective leading operations, I found that vulnerability is a key element to influence and establish discipline. The more discipline I can establish for myself, the more credibility I can establish as an individual, the more that transcends the entire team, and the more consistent we can be. Simon Sinek uses the example of brushing your teeth. If we brush our teeth twice a day, once a week, we'll never have clean teeth. We have to do it twice a day, every day. We have to incorporate that consistency. That's the same thing with leadership. Doing things every so often will not influence or create discipline in our teams, but if we can incorporate these things every day, that's how we generate high-level momentum.

Vulnerability has been a key part of my experience, which includes knowing how to admit mistakes to our teammates and knowing the selective times to share important information that can be helpful to them. Vulnerability makes us relatable and can carry influence. For example, if a leader had a substance abuse issue, and they admitted that and what they did to overcome it to a teammate who's also going through it, they can help them. All these great, powerful things influence and empower that team member to get over it, as opposed to judging it or stigmatizing that behavior, which makes that situation harder for that teammate to overcome.

Overall, discipline is a powerful tool to maintain a positive outlook and get everyone to understand that adversity will come for all of us. But we can overcome anything if we can maintain a disciplined and positive mindset.

Resilience is a fundamental part of my life. I've spent most of my life, whether subconsciously or intentionally, working to develop higher levels of resilience in my life and career. I've had a lot of missteps and failings in my life. One that sticks out to me is using alcohol to self-medicate stress from highly stressful work environments. As somebody who grew up not being exposed to substance abuse and then going into the military at a young age and being around the drinking culture, drinking became something I could do when things got hard and stressful. I used alcohol to cope. And it was a maladaptive and unhealthy way to do that. However, those experiences helped me form some understanding of humility and resilience and how to pick yourself up and push through internal shame. Shame held me back the most—the feelings of imperfection and insecurities to admit that I don't know as much as I think I do or I'm not as squared away as I think I am.

Those are powerful lessons in developing humility and resilience. Because guess what? The same person who was abusing alcohol is the same person who is a business owner and writing a book and speaking publicly on these issues; it's the same person. What changed was the response after the incident. We all have situations and adverse experiences that cause us to falter and fail. That is going to happen for all of us. The question is, what do you do when that happens?

I licked my wounds for eighteen months. I had to find a way to pick myself up once I came to grips with the fact that I needed to change my life. But at the end of the day, we have to take action and understand who we are. We have to evaluate our values. We have to look at the relationship capital in our lives. Who are the most important people in our lives that we need to get ourselves healthy for? And then we need to ask them, what do you need from me? Then, we need to be accountable and hold ourselves to the highest standards.

As a man, I wanted my family to depend on me. I didn't want to have to be the one they had to pick up, nurture, and hold. I want to be that man and rock for my family. That's important to me. When I knew what I wanted to do, it became a matter of charting a path forward to get there. Sometimes, the confusion of where we want to go holds us back. We all have an ability once it's inside of us and we know where we want to go to make a plan. So don't focus so much on the misstep as much as the future and where you want to go. Once you do that, resilience starts to take hold as you push through your shame and make that plan to attack. Each one of us has something special to do. We can overcome and develop disciplined and resilient mindsets, which help us become the most influential leaders and affect every aspect of our companies and organizations.

ACTION STEPS

1. Develop a Strong Sense of Discipline: The author emphasizes the importance of discipline in navigating career changes and entrepreneurial challenges. In your business, this could mean setting clear goals and consistently working towards them. It involves understanding your strengths and weaknesses, and leveraging this self-awareness to make informed decisions. By staying disciplined, you maintain focus on your business objectives, which can lead to sustained growth and success.

2. Foster Resilience in the Face of Challenges: Resilience is highlighted as a key trait for dealing with business obstacles. In your case, this could mean viewing challenges not as setbacks but as opportunities for growth. This approach involves embracing failure, learning from it, and using these lessons to strengthen your business strategy. Developing resilience can help

you navigate the ups and downs of business with a steady hand, ensuring long-term sustainability and adaptability.

3. Practice Personal Accountability and Leadership: The author stresses the importance of personal accountability and leading by example. For your business, this means holding yourself to the highest standards and being the first to admit and learn from mistakes. By doing so, you set a strong example for your team, fostering a culture of accountability and positive influence. This approach can enhance team performance, build trust, and create a work environment where everyone strives for excellence.

About the Author

Chad M. Bruckner is an entrepreneur and motivational speaker from Allentown, PA. Chad served thirteen years in law enforcement in multiple roles such as patrolman, detective, and undercover officer. Chad served eight years in the US Army Infantry and led combat missions in Iraq. Chad is a passionate advocate for veterans and police officers. Chad's mission is to inspire and empower first responders and veterans to reach their full potential. Chad has developed training programs in wellness, leadership, and resiliency; and publicly speaks on these issues. Chad is guided by his faith and core values and has dedicated his life to serving others. Chad holds a master's degree in digital forensics and a bachelor's degree in criminal justice. Chad is married to the love of his life, Kristen, and they have three children. Chad loves Philly sports, music, and film. Connect with Chad on socials!

Daily Disciplines: The Key to Character Development

Jon Hoerauf

During the final year of my undergraduate degree, I opted to move out of the dormitory to cut costs. I leased the basement of a wonderful older lady whom I affectionately referred to as Grandma.

Each evening, I would head upstairs to join her for a session of watching Wheel Of Fortune and engage in some conversation before returning to the basement. My apartment was essentially an open space with a sink and a small refrigerator. Lacking a stove, I relied on an electric frypan and a slow cooker to prepare my meals. While my diet mainly consisted of mac and cheese, I occasionally treated myself to chicken and rice.

By nature, I'm not inclined to plan, so when left to my own devices, I typically rely on my memory and create mental lists. Given the intangibility of these lists, I repeatedly review them to organize the information and ensure I haven't overlooked anything. However, it was during this phase of my life that I realized the shortcomings of this organizational method. I discovered that such habits often resulted in forgetting crucial tasks, misplacing essential documents, and missing important deadlines.

One night, as I lay in bed, mentally juggling the tasks for the upcoming day and yearning for a restful sleep, I had an epiphany—I needed to change my approach. Taking out a piece of paper, I meticulously listed everything that needed attention the next day. The surprising outcome was a sense of relief.

With the tasks neatly outlined on paper, ready to tackle upon waking, I could release my concerns and peacefully drift off to sleep. After that revelation, crafting a list of the next day's tasks became integral to my nightly routine.

I discovered that assuming control of my schedule, even though it initially felt contrary to my nature, brought about a sense of freedom. Despite discipline inherently being a form of self-constraint, it ultimately paves the way for greater freedom in the long run. This holds true whether applied to maintaining your finances, exercising regularly, or attending to essential tasks crucial for the smooth operation of your business.

Suppose discipline involves addressing the present moment and carrying out necessary tasks even when not in the mood. In that case, consistency is the key that turns discipline into a lasting lifestyle change. Once you set a goal, you'll identify several new disciplines necessary for turning that goal into a reality. However, your goal will remain unrealized unless these disciplines are consistently applied over an extended period. Achieving change demands persistent effort dedicated to cultivating new habits over time.

Every individual possesses character, and this character undergoes evolution, either for the better or worse. The determining factor in the direction of your character growth is the consistency of your daily actions. Goals represent what you aspire to become, and disciplines represent the necessary actions to achieve those goals. However, it is your daily, consistent actions that ultimately shape the type of character you develop.

To cultivate consistent, positive behavior, one must focus on self-reflection rather than external influences. If you regularly gauge others' responses to your actions, adjusting your course based on either their microexpressions or overt responses, you risk living solely to please or appease others.

However, by directing your focus inward—toward understanding who you are or who you aspire to be—you will naturally make decisions that align with this self-image. In a world marked by comparison and competition, whether through entertainment, social media, or professional development goals at work, constantly evaluating our perceived value often steers our focus outward rather than on internal growth.

Shifting our attention toward internal growth empowers us to establish personal goals, identify the necessary disciplines to achieve them, and, when consistently practiced, cultivate positive character traits. This way of living liberates individuals from the shackles of comparison to others and external standards, paving the way for them to become their personal best.

Behaving consistently over an extended period requires endurance. While there are likely various theories on where to find or how to increase endurance, for our purposes, I want to concentrate on two sources: grit-based endurance and identity-based passion.

Everyone possesses a certain level of innate grit. This quality enables you to endure driving through a snowstorm all night to return home or persevere through a demanding season with insufficient sleep. Whether during a new product launch or following a key employee's change in position, the rest of the team must unite to handle an augmented workload. The emotions stirred by the "crisis" prompt you to tap into untapped reservoirs of creativity and strength. You might be astonished by the reserve you can access when needed.

Nevertheless, there is a limit to this strength. Sustaining such a high activity level will inevitably result in burnout because the source of this strength is our own stored resources. It's imperative to rest, refresh, and replenish our reserves, allowing us to resume work effectively. Businesses that neglect their employees' needs typically witness diminished output, disgruntled workers, and increased turnover. In most situations, when grit-based endurance is required, individuals can swiftly tap into their reserves and perform at a supercharged level—at least for a time.

On the other hand, identity-based passion stems far deeper and more abundant than our own grit. It takes considerably longer to develop than grit-based endurance but is inherently self-rejuvenating and appears limitless in its resources. Identity-based endurance emanates from an internal fountain nourished by a belief system.

No matter how you present yourself outwardly, if deep down you harbor the belief that you are an imposter merely attempting to conform to a role, your wellspring of endurance will rapidly diminish, requiring reliance on sheer determination to navigate the day. Conversely, by aligning your belief system with your genuine desires, you can access an inexhaustible source of energy.

For example, consider a scenario where you oversee a team, whether it comprises three or three hundred individuals. While everyone around you perceives you as a competent leader, internally, you believe your position resulted from chance. If others could discern your true self, they would immediately replace you. In the daily routine, when your team operates smoothly with minimal intervention, you might convince yourself that you are an effective leader.

However, one day, your supervisor informs you that one of your staff members lost their temper with another colleague. This occurred in front of customers to compound the issue, who subsequently brought it to the supervisor's attention. You are tasked with addressing this situation. It isn't a quick-fix scenario, as you need to determine the underlying reasons for the first staff member losing their temper and ensure that the other staff member feels supported. Additionally, you must handle any repercussions from this incident with your customers.

If you see yourself as an imposter, your instinct may be to quash this feeling swiftly. You might lack the stamina to confront this challenging issue head-on. You could opt to promptly address the responsible individual, instructing them not to repeat their actions, or you might sidestep the situation, hoping it resolves itself. In either case, you are not addressing the actual problem, as your belief in your inadequacy prevents you from tackling it effectively.

Yet, suppose you have confronted your imposter syndrome over time and reshaped your belief system to acknowledge that you are a leader for a reason, possessing the capabilities to handle difficult situations. In that case, your approach will be markedly different. You will no longer perceive the two employees as a problem to be fixed but rather as two individuals deserving of support.

Your passion for becoming an influential and effective leader will embolden you to engage in a challenging conversation with the first staff member. Instead of solely seeking to impose discipline, you will aim to provide support and encouragement for their growth. You will invest time in understanding what happened and the reasons behind their behavior.

Furthermore, your profound passion for effective leadership will channel your energy toward the well-being of all players involved in this scenario. This determination will give you the endurance and capability to overcome obstacles, enabling you to see the situation through to its resolution, even when it requires stepping outside your comfort zone.

I begin every day with a quiet moment at home. Once I step into my office, my focus shifts to catching up on emails, conducting meetings, or working on projects. If I miss my quiet time at home, it rarely happens later. I shoot for thirty to forty-five minutes every morning, though sometimes it's only feasible to carve out fifteen minutes to calm my mind and set a positive tone for the day.

My dedicated spot at home, accompanied by a cup of coffee, is where I cherish this time, not in the car en route to work or amidst potential distractions. Typically, I read my Bible during this period, finding it incredibly uplifting and grounding. Commencing the day with an eternal perspective prevents me from being overly entangled in daily drama. Occasionally, if the sunrise is particularly beautiful, I take my coffee to the backyard, marvel at the scenery, and let gratitude and awe wash over me.

Throughout the day, I try to replicate moments of stillness, allowing myself to momentarily transcend this present reality and exist in a higher state where time, deadlines, and the approval of others are irrelevant. I relish these moments of peace and rest, and then, rejuvenated, I return to the task at hand.

It's hard to admit, but I've allowed our constantly connected digital world to exert more control over my life than it should.

In my professional life, communication primarily revolves around email and Microsoft Teams. While these tools can be invaluable, it's all too easy for them to shift from being helpful tools to becoming masters dictating my every move.

Frequent interruptions from pop-ups on my computer, signaling new emails or messages, have become a constant source of distraction. Despite my efforts to resist the urge to check immediately, there's a persistent inner voice urging me to verify, just in case something crucial requires immediate attention. Even when away from my desk, I catch myself reflexively glancing at my phone, anticipating a new message.

Although I've attempted to limit email checks to specific times, adhering to this plan has proven tricky. Implementing it would involve turning off reminders for both email and Teams and finding a practical way to manage communication without constant alerts. To address this, I've decided to take occasional breaks from my desk, bringing my laptop to a quiet location to work. In support of this effort, I've disabled Teams notifications on my phone to remain unaware of incoming messages. During these focused work sessions, I closed my email on the computer and turned my phone upside down, creating an environment free from distractions and allowing me to concentrate on tasks more effectively.

Balancing the spectrum of consistency and adaptability is a natural process for any living organism, and the same holds true for a business. Excessive emphasis on consistency can render your business rigid, losing relevance to an ever-evolving clientele. Conversely, a disproportionate focus on adaptability may lead to frustration and exhaustion among your workforce, giving clients the impression that your business lacks an actual direction.

In essence, I believe the key to maintaining balance is having a clear vision. It is crucial to remain consistent in principles and character while fostering nimble adaptability in your practices. Vision facilitates this delicate equilibrium. By addressing questions such as why you exist and the ultimate impact you aim to make, you establish a sturdy framework upon which to build. This framework remains steadfast, even in companies with a long history.

What you incorporate into that framework can and should evolve to align with the current climate, but the foundation remains secure. Consider an old house in a historic district. While the foundation, layout, and structure remain unchanged from when it was first built 150 years ago, the external features have likely undergone several transformations. The house may have had multiple new roofs and received several coats of paint, and perhaps the original plaster walls have been replaced with drywall. Some exterior elements, like molding or a wraparound porch, may have experienced rot and needed replacement—but the stone foundation and wood frame are the same as always.

A house of this nature can retain the awe-inspiring beauty of its original design while being equipped with modernized electrical, plumbing, and internet networking. Recently, I heard about a local business that has been operating for over 150 years. Although their fundamental customer base and vision remain consistent, I'm sure that their processes have undergone multiple updates and improvements since they first opened their doors. The guiding factor in this enduring success is vision.

Your company's vision is intricately tied to the organization's personality rather than solely focused on the products or services you offer. Years ago, I came across a story about a man employed in the railroad industry. One scorching summer day, as he and a coworker were repairing a section of tracks, the CEO of the railroad passed by and greeted the man by name. The worker paused his task for a brief conversation with the CEO. Upon resuming his work, his coworker was amazed that he knew the CEO and inquired about the encounter.

The man explained that he and the CEO commenced their careers at the railroad nearly thirty years ago. This naturally led to the question, "Why is he the CEO while you're still doing physical labor?" The man responded, "I have always been in the train business, but he's been in the transportation business."

In the early stages of my career, I served as a counselor at a residential facility for teenagers. These boys were removed from their communities for various legal reasons and lived on campus for about a year, during which we endeavored to assist them in healing and preparing for their return home. As expected, not all of them were the most likable individuals. I distinctly recall one young man who would persistently challenge my authority, attempt to exploit any opportunity for misbehavior, and consistently evade personal responsibility for his actions. Over the weeks, my feelings toward this individual soured, and the anticipation of encountering him made me dread going to work.

One day, right after lunch, he reverted to his usual pattern of refusing to comply with my instructions. Whether driven by my frustration, pride, or the power dynamics in our relationship, I escalated the situation to the point where he had to be restrained by a couple of other staff members and me. Once the dust settled, a sense of remorse overwhelmed me. Throughout the night, I reflected on the incident, and the following day, I took him aside and offered a sincere apology for my actions. I acknowledged that the conflict didn't need to reach such intensity and took responsibility for the escalation, admitting that it was my fault.

At that moment, I resolved to find a way to appreciate him. I initiated a search for positive traits, constantly highlighting them in my mind. I made a deliberate effort to observe and acknowledge the positive aspects of his actions. While I couldn't overlook his negative behaviors, when it became necessary to address them, I approached him as a valuable individual rather than dismissing him as an aggressive troublemaker.

Intentionally altering my mindset toward this person significantly impacted our relationship and positively influenced his progress through our program. Yet, the most surprising revelation was the transformation within me. I realized that I actually did like him. What had started as a decision developed into a belief and eventually became my reality. This shift even elevated my job satisfaction.

During this period, I began to realize my mindset's significant influence on my emotions, habits, and beliefs. Since then, I've applied this principle to various aspects of my life, encompassing both personal and professional disciplines.

I've come to understand the importance of honest and deep self-reflection. Uncovering one's belief system can be challenging because it often feels normal. For instance, just as you instinctively look down to find a dropped pen due to your belief in gravity, certain beliefs about yourself and others are deeply ingrained. Messages received during upbringing, such as being inferior to siblings or classmates, become embedded in your belief system, much like the unquestioned acceptance of gravity.

When pursuing goals like obtaining a degree or seeking a promotion, negative thoughts rooted in these beliefs, such as I'm not smart enough or They already have someone else in mind can undermine efforts. Instead of actively acquiring new skills, individuals may settle for their perceived limitations.

Changing self-perception is a complex process. Discovering and altering negative beliefs about oneself and others provides the motivation and discipline to pursue one's destiny. The willingness to hold oneself accountable is a matter of pride, often stemming from fear. The imposter syndrome, where one feels inadequate despite external success, can lead to defensive behavior. Focusing on proving one's worth detracts from the primary work objective, resulting in disproportionate energy spent on maintaining a facade rather than fulfilling job responsibilities.

Defensiveness in the face of correction or questioning hinders personal growth and accountability. Those who avoid accountability may react defensively to protect a perceived weakness. Exploring and challenging these beliefs is crucial for personal and professional development.

Leadership is pivotal in fostering a culture of discipline within a team. The leader's accountability sets the standards for the team. Hiring the right individuals is essential, but the team may lower its standards if the leader isn't modeling personal discipline. Leaders must define valuable disciplines for the organization, model them, and expect adherence from the team.

Discipline extends beyond punctuality and focus to encompass values like having fun at work, ensuring customer satisfaction, and maintaining work-life balance. Leaders determine organizational values and maintaining them requires dedication and consistency.

ACTION STEPS

1.   Implement a Daily Planning Routine: Just like the author found relief in writing down tasks, you can improve your business by starting each day with a clear plan. This could involve listing your top priorities, setting specific goals for the day, or outlining steps for ongoing projects. By doing this, you ensure that important tasks don't slip through the cracks and that your day is structured efficiently.

2.   Develop Consistent, Positive Behaviors in Your Team: The chapter stresses the importance of consistency in character development. You can apply this by encouraging consistent, positive behaviors within your team. For example, you might establish regular training sessions, encourage employees to set personal growth goals, or create a system for recognizing and rewarding consistent performance. This approach will help develop a team that is reliable and continuously improving.

3.   Balance Grit with Identity-Based Passion: The chapter discusses the limits of grit-based endurance and the sustainability of identity-based passion. In your business, encourage a culture where employees connect their personal values and passions with their work. This could involve open discussions about personal and professional goals, creating roles that align with individual strengths and passions, and encouraging a work environment where personal identity is valued. This approach will likely lead to a more engaged and resilient workforce, capable of tackling challenges with enthusiasm and persistence.

ABOUT THE AUTHOR

Jon Hoerauf has a background as a counselor and teacher. He is a writer and professional speaker in the areas of motivation, leadership, and teamwork. To schedule him for a workshop or as a keynote speaker, you can contact him at jon@JonHoerauf.com.

Dear Entrepreneur,

Are you looking for a way to take your business to the next level? Writing a co-authored book could be the answer you've been searching for.

As an entrepreneur, you know the importance of building an authoritative presence in your industry. When you co-author a book, it adds instant credibility to your name and opens the door to increased influence and networking opportunities.

That's why SAB Publishing is excited to offer you this unique opportunity. Co-authoring a book with us gives you the chance to become a bestselling author and increase your lead flow. Plus, you'll be able to build your brand and grow your business.

At SAB Publishing, we understand the needs of entrepreneurs like you. That's why we make it easy to write a co-authored book with us. An experienced publisher and editor helps you write a compelling story, as well as professional design and marketing services.

Take the first step to becoming a bestselling author and growing your business.

Contact SAB Publishing today (jetlaunch.link/sp) to learn more about our co-authoring opportunities to grow your business.

Chris O'Byrne
SAB Publishing
books@strategicadvisorboard.com

SAB
PUBLISHING

www.ingramcontent.com/pod-product-compliance
Lightning Source LLC
Chambersburg PA
CBHW031400180326
41458CB00043B/6551/J